WOMEN CHANGE
the WORLD

WOMEN CHANGE
the WORLD

*Noteworthy Women on Cultivating Your
Potential and Achieving Success*

Edited by Michelle Patterson

BenBella Books, Inc.
Dallas, Texas

BenBella

BenBella Books, Inc.
10300 N. Central Expressway, Suite 530
Dallas, TX 75231
www.benbellabooks.com
Send feedback to feedback@benbellabooks.com

Printed in the United States of America
10 9 8 7 6 5 4 3 2 1

Library of Congress Cataloging-in-Publication
Data is available for this title.
978-1-939529-17-6

Copyediting by Debra Kirkby, Kirkby Editorial Services
Proofreading by Jenny Bridges and Chris Gage
Cover design by Kara Davidson, Faceout Studios
Text design by Silver Feather Design
Text composition by Integra Software Services Private Limited
Printed by Bang Printing

Distributed by Perseus Distribution
(www.perseusdistribution.com)

To place orders through Perseus Distribution:
Tel: 800-343-4499
Fax: 800-351-5073
E-mail: orderentry@perseusbooks.com

Significant discounts for bulk sales are available. Please contact Glenn
Yeffeth at glenn@benbellabooks.com or 214-750-3628.

contents

Michelle *Patterson's*
name conjures up many credits—visionary, author, acceleration executive, founder, passionate, talk show host, and dynamic speaker. She is a woman of many dimensions.

Today, Michelle Patterson is president of the Global Women Foundation, a 501(c)(3) public charity that serves to provide support, leadership, and advocacy for women's initiatives around the globe. The charity, which started almost ten years ago as a local festival supporting twenty-two charities, has grown into a global movement for women.

Michelle is also the founder, president, and CEO of Women Network LLC, a digital media company giving women a voice to share their message. WomenNetwork .com's "umbrella platform" shines a light on organizations and corporations that empower women and brings them together as a community to experience the Women Network's motto: "We Are Better Together." The online digital network provides women resources, tools, and advice to achieve their full potential.

Michelle is driven by the belief that everyone has something significant to contribute and that when people (male or female) come together and support one another, we truly are better together. She is committed to helping individuals discover their talent and connect with the right circle of people to live out their purpose.

Michelle Patterson had the good fortune to interview California governor George Deukmejian when she was twelve-years-old. Governor Deukmejian was just starting the

California Women's Conference to advance women's causes. Nearly thirty years later, Michelle took over the reins of the well-known California Women's Conference, continuing its twenty-eight-year tradition as the nation's preeminent conference for women—a perfect example of the objective Governor Deukmejian set out when he first started the conference.

Michelle is a successful event promoter (Taste of Ladera), a lauded business accelerator (youngest regional vice president and national sales trainer for Robert Half, the world's largest specialized recruiting firm), a sought-after media commentator (the *Huffington Post*, CNBC, Fox Business News, Bloomberg, and dozens of California television stations), an energetic and engaging public speaker, and host of a weekly radio show on Women Network Talk Radio.

Beyond her notable business success, Michelle is most passionate about her family. She lives in Ladera Ranch, California, with Eric, her husband of nearly twenty years and a successful corporate CFO in his own right, and their two beautiful children, Jaclyn and Chase.

Introduction

Warren Buffett says he is excited about the state of the economy as we are just now beginning to tap into the other 50 percent of the talent pool—the female half. The full potential of women will finally be unleashed and the world has no idea what we're in for!

Every conversation I have with women always revolves around their need to be a part of something greater than themselves. They are just looking for encouragement and support that will enable them to change the world. As Steve Jobs said, "The ones who are crazy enough to think that they can change the world are the ones who do."

That's where my story starts—with doing something I never thought I would do.

In 2009, as the recession hit and the economy slowed down, the state of California decided to cut funding for the California Women's Conference. A program that had been going on for thirty years would stop abruptly. That's when I started getting calls. I was one of two women in the state who was already producing large-scale charity events.

Taking on Governor George Deukmejian's legacy was no easy task. With months of preparation, I signed up thousands of attendees, brought in more than 250 exhibitors, and secured more than 150 speakers. Things were off to a great start, but as the event grew closer, not all went according to the plan. Funding fell through on the project and, with only seventeen days until the event, I was $1.8 million in the hole. The event was in danger of being cancelled.

The event had to go on! Thousands of people were expecting to attend; thousands of women needed the resources this conference provides. Shutting down was not an option. So I did the only thing I knew how to do: I checked my ego in at the door and asked for help.

Together with the support of family, friends, and my advisors, I went from cancelling the event and filing for bankruptcy to reducing what was owed from $1.8 million to $150,000.

The event went on and it was a great success! That's when I knew I wanted to take that moment and create a movement.

When I initially took on producing the California Women's Conference, I had no idea what I was in for. The event offers its attendees inspiration, resources, and connections to take the next steps in their businesses, personal development, or philanthropic endeavors, but it taught me a powerful lesson: what happens when we come together and help each other instead of working independently.

With that in mind, I founded the Global Women Foundation, with our motto: "WE ARE BETTER TOGETHER."

The Global Women Foundation is a natural extension of the historic California Women's Conference. When the Conference began twenty-eight years ago, then-governor George Deukmejian's primary objective was to address the failure rate of women in business in California. Today, our objective for the Global Women Foundation is to harness the passion and ambition the conference embodies and take it around the globe. It is our mission to build a global community of women, men, organizations, and governments that share our vision, and provide a forum for people who share our passion to address issues important to women.

When we sit down with women from all over the world, I realize that we are all the same inside. We are all looking for ways to connect and bring our organizations together because truly, we are better together.

Over the past year, I have traveled around the United States, handpicking those who I believe are world-changing women and inviting them to participate in this movement—to be a part of the California Women's Conference and this book. From actresses, motivational speakers, and writers to businesswomen and other high-profile female professionals, this book focuses on women's unique contributions to society. The overall goal is to highlight, through stories and experiences, women's contributions to their own and others' success, as well as to empower readers to go out and change the world themselves. Each one of these essays started as an interview, but as we got to know each other better, I realized this movement is even bigger than I initially thought.

Through this book and the California Women's Conference, my vision is to create a community where women are told that they matter and that their contributions are important.

Learn from my experience and from the experiences of my friends, who also share their stories in this book. See how you can get involved and make a difference, too.

WOMEN CHANGE
the WORLD

JoAnn Albers is the founder of Albers Consulting, LLC, of Portland, Oregon, which aids nonprofits in fund-raising, communications and marketing, board and leadership development, event planning, and other aspects of running a successful organization. Since 1992, her efforts on behalf of Doernbecher Children's Hospital in Portland have netted $40 million. She helped Oregon Health and Science University, as a member of the OHSU Foundation board, to raise more than $300 million and to establish the nationally renowned OHSU Women's Health Center.

Fund-raising is a great field for women because I think the playing field is very level, whether you are staff or working in development or consulting. Women's opportunities for success are equal to men's.

As for myself, I've never had a problem working with men because men tend to be more direct in the way they communicate and more singular in their focus, and I am that way, too. I do think it is important to recognize the differences between the sexes, though. As a strategist, I take those differences into account when I analyze a situation and plan how I am going to achieve the end result I am looking for. I don't look at gender differences as negative things; I just incorporate them into my strategy for achieving a positive solution.

It's fairly common for me to be invited to tackle relationship issues or personal conflicts in fund-raising—issues involving both male and female donors. I think what I have been able to do as a woman is to see things from a different perspective and to relate to women on an emotional level. I have developed a lot of solid relationships with women, whether they were board members or staff.

I developed skills for working with teams and organizations at an early age. I grew up in a family of ten kids, and I am the third child and oldest daughter. I learned as a child how to be part of a team or a community because that's the only way our family could function properly.

I don't have a college education. I had a full scholarship offered to me based on financial need and academic achievement. However, my parents were from the generation that wondered why a girl would want to go to college unless she wanted to be a teacher or a nurse. I didn't want to be either, so instead of going to college, I married a Catholic boy. Yet I have done well without a degree because what I did have was the drive to be successful. All the people I worked with in the fund-raising firm in which I came up had master's degrees.

I was the marketing person, and not having a degree did not stop me from increasing their business 42 percent in three years.

I do think that women can accomplish great things together. I have lent my fund-raising skills to the Orange County Women's Philanthropy Fund, which is part of United Way. That is a powerful group of women. Ten years ago, we established a "circle of giving." A lot of men didn't think women could be successful in doing this, but it is working all around the country in groups called Women in Philanthropy. These groups together have raised close to $1 billion. All the women in these groups support and respect each other and their missions, financially and in the time they give.

One very important way to support other women is to mentor those who are starting out. I think we have an obligation to give back by helping younger women develop the skill sets they need to move into upper management, and I love doing it.

The first thing I'd say to a woman starting out in her professional career is, "Don't be afraid of being successful." After that, find out what you need to do to achieve a balance between work life and home life. That is one of the most difficult challenges in my own life and career, but finding that balance is important to our lives, our companies, our families—even our health. So we need a solid support system based on our family, our friends, and other women we meet professionally.

Jane Applegate is one of America's leading experts on small-business management. She's the author of four books, including *201 Great Ideas for Your Small Business* (Bloomberg/Wiley). The Applegate Group Inc. is a multimedia production company specializing in producing sponsored content for small-business owners. Current and past clients include Plum Alley, Microsoft, American Express, Cox Business, and Bloomberg LP. A former syndicated small-business columnist for the *Los Angeles Times*, Jane is currently producing two films about strong women. She is the cofounder of FabulousFemaleNetwork.com.

There are many women journalists, but being an investigative reporter—for the *Los Angeles Times*—was a challenge. I was the first full-time white-collar crime reporter for the *Los Angeles Times*. It was a dangerous beat, given that I was writing about criminals, but it was very exciting. My breaking-news stories frequently appeared on the front page.

Being a woman in financial journalism was an asset when I was interviewing high-powered male executives who considered me young and naïve. Many top executives at the companies I was covering would share way more details and information than I asked for, leading me to ask better and more probing questions. Michael Milken, formerly with Drexel Burnham Lambert, made headlines as the "junk bond king" and was later convicted of securities fraud. I like to think my reporting helped put him behind bars.

I have really only had one significant experience in my career when being a woman caused me grief. I was working at the *San Diego Union* in the early 1980s, when I asked for a part-time reporting job after the birth of my twins in 1981. The editor denied the request and the Newspaper Guild (union) refused to back me, so I packed up my possessions and resigned from the paper. A few days later, the editor called and finally offered me a three-day workweek. However, as punishment for being a "troublemaker," I was exiled to a remote bureau about thirty miles from my home, where my beat was to cover the rural areas of San Diego County. I wrote several front-page feature stories about casinos on Indian reservations and the life of a cattle rancher. Working so far from home made it more difficult to balance work and family, despite my part-time schedule.

However, I was determined to succeed, so I worked extra hours on the weekends to hone my writing skills. A few months and a few front-page stories later, I was hired by the *Los Angeles Times*. So much for being exiled from the newsroom!

At my newspaper and television jobs, I always seemed to work longer hours than the men, despite having young children. I was lucky to be married to Joe Applegate. He was a copy editor with a set late-afternoon-into-evening schedule. His career accommodated my need to work flexible hours. I accepted every assignment, traveled frequently, and never expected my employers to give me special treatment because I was a working mother. When I signed my first book contract in 1991, I quit the *Times* to start my own communications/video and film production company. Being an entrepreneur provided me with more control over my time and a significant boost in my income. It was a very good career move.

Working so hard led to a fantastic career—including awards for my writing and filmmaking, national speaking tours, four books, and a life that is never boring. I've produced a variety of television programs, events, and promotional videos. Now, I'm producing two feature films—both about strong women. I'm also consulting with a great new company, Plum Alley, that crowd-funds projects for women and sells upscale merchandise on a beautiful e-commerce platform.

I've been successful based on working long hours and my passion for telling stories, which I don't think are gender-specific traits. But I do think there are differences between men and women that matter in the workplace. I think women are better listeners than men. Our ability to multitask is also essential to meeting tight deadlines and juggling several projects at once. I covered breaking news most of my career and thrived on the pressure of meeting daily deadlines.

I've always admired Barbara Walters for being a pioneer in my field, but I never had a female mentor myself. All my mentors—until recently—were men. Now I'm working with several female producers and directors who are collaborating on and supporting my projects. I'm mentoring my daughter, Jeanne, an independent film editor who quit her job at Pixar to pursue her dreams. I've also made it a point to mentor young women who worked for my company as writers and producers. Today, one is a senior producer at CBS News and the other is a successful development producer at a TV production company.

The best advice I can give a young woman starting out? Stand by your word and be accountable for your actions. To be truly successful and happy, never work with anyone who gives you a headache or a stomachache. There are so many wonderful, talented people out there. Choose your collaborators and colleagues wisely.

Janet Bray Attwood is the coauthor of the *New York Times* best-seller *The Passion Test: The Effortless Path to Discovering Your Life Purpose,* and the coauthor of *From Sad to Glad: 7 Steps to Facing Change with Love and Power.* She has appeared as a featured speaker before hundreds of thousands of people around the world, sharing the podium with the Dalai Lama, Sir Richard Branson, T. Harv Eker, Jack Canfield, Lisa Nichols, Stephen Covey, and Brendon Burchard, among others.

Janet has received the President's Volunteer Service Award for her work with the homeless and children in lockdown detention centers. Janet has worked in the corporate world as marketing director for Books Are Fun, the third largest book buyer in the US. Janet is a teacher of Transcendental Meditation and is past president of The World United, an organization in India that promotes healthy and sustainable choices for a better world. She is on the international advisory board for the Centre for Management in Mumbai, which offers business degrees and promotes international business qualifications. She is a Dane, knighted by the order of St. John for her humanitarian work.

I've been asked to comment here about the special traits and talents that women have, but to tell you the truth, I never think of myself as living in a separate world from men. I really look at the world in terms of the unity of us all. I don't mean that women and men aren't different in any way, just that each of us needs to discover who we are and what our passions are, and align our lives with that discovery. In that sense, I am constantly using the knowledge that I share with others to be the best person I can be and to express my feminine power.

There are certainly challenges related to being a woman. I just returned from a trip through China and Japan. I visit a lot of places where it is still very much a man's world, although even in these cultures women are making great inroads. Being on stage, as I so often am, is not an inherently feminine role; commanding a whole audience can be very masculine in terms of energy.

Another challenge is that I can't just rely on my innate feminine skills and be a transformational leader all the time. I also have to employ marketing skills, meaning I had to learn how to switch on parts of my brain that were dormant to keep up in this masculine, competitive world.

And yet, in the work I do, I can be as feminine as I want, presenting myself as a woman with a great message—and I can do that standing next to some of the most powerful men on the planet and feel that I am collaborating with them, not competing. Also, what I do depends on being a person who people are willing to listen to and follow—so my intuition, my feminine ability to tap into that inner knowledge, probably gives me an edge.

I always function more on a level of feeling and intuition. My approach to getting things done has a softer side to it. As I travel around the world, I really zero in on what people are looking for at a very deep, emotional level. People come to my events to gain deep knowledge. They want to be noticed, to know that they have value, and to truly be touched and to have it be a straight-to-the-heart experience.

In the end, though, being a woman is just a part of who I am, and that is who I have to be. I can't compete with my male friends like Jack Canfield and Les Brown because I can't be who they are. We all just need to allow ourselves to be the best that we can be. Collaboration is the name of the game. We are not in it to compete but to bring out each other's greatness. We are here to give each person a chance to shine.

One my dearest friends is Marci Shimoff, the *New York Times* bestselling author of eight books who was featured in the hit film *The Secret*, and I have also recently gotten to know the spiritual teacher and activist Marianne Williamson. These are women who have stepped out of that world of competition, who come from that very centered and feminine place. Yet they reach an audience of both women and men because they are so crystal clear in delivering their message. Their femininity is like a magnet to people. I think of the poet Maya Angelou that way, too.

The point is that women are in the unique position of drawing out the best in people. We all grow the most when we're surrounded by people who create a good and positive influence on us. As a woman, that is how I see the world. I absolutely believe that every moment is a gift. There are no mistakes in the universe, so it isn't up to me to say this was good and that was bad, this was right and that was wrong. I believe seeing connections more clearly allows us to appreciate and value all the experiences of our lives.

There was a moment in my life when I had a true revelation. Before I created the Passion Test process, now the number one tool used globally to discover passion and connect with purpose, I was stuck in a job where I was failing miserably. I was a recruiter of computer engineers in Silicon Valley, and I was just awful at it. I had no passion for it, and I had trouble understanding what my clients wanted because I didn't understand the language of this primarily male, analytical world of disk drive engineers.

I began to realize that I was here to do something great, but I wasn't yet doing it. I remembered my mother telling me, "Janet, you are here for greatness." One night when I was despairing about my failures at work, I went to meditate at the local meditation center—I had been practicing Transcendental Meditation (TM) for years. On the wall I saw a sign advertising a success seminar in San Francisco. I had been praying for a sign, and I told myself this was the one I was looking for. The next morning, I called in sick to work, drove to San Francisco, walked into that seminar, and sat down in the front row. The woman teaching the program was so happy, centered, and crystal clear it was amazing. Everything about her seemed perfect.

She was an incredible role model for me. I could feel that she was aligned from the inside out and I wanted that. Right then, I realized that being a transformational speaker was what I was meant to do.

As I began my journey into the world of transformation, I learned that the secret to being really happy is in giving, in being of service to others. One of the clearest examples was when I first started the Passion Test program. I got an e-mail from a group in Miami that was working with homeless women. They told me they were organizing an event and would be busing in two hundred homeless women. They were going to feed them on china and give them all kinds of presents, and they wanted me to come and share the Passion Test with them. They said they couldn't pay me.

At that time, I was in the Midwest, which meant I'd have to travel a long way at my own expense, but I listened to my heart, and I knew I didn't have a choice but to get on that plane. I went to Miami and spoke to the homeless women. As I stood on the stage interacting with these precious women who had gone through so much, I realized I wasn't the one giving. I was the one receiving. That was the most important talk I had given. In that moment I realized that these women were no different than anyone else on the planet, and in fact, all they'd been through made them more open, more appreciative, and more ready to change than most of my audiences.

That night inspired me to create the Empowered Women's Series, a monthly program designed to inspire, uplift, and motivate women in transition all over the United States. I brought together great people like Lisa Nichols and created a whole CD series that is sent out free to anyone running a homeless shelter or detention center. This wasn't anything I was going to make money on. It just felt like the right thing to do, and I did it. As a woman, I could feel for these women so deeply and I believe that as women we have a responsibility to uplift and support one another.

Another time, I was on a plane coming home from India when an Indian woman struck up a conversation. What caught her interest was that I was making jewelry on the plane. As it happened, she ran an organization in Bangalore to help 25,000 indigent women escape beatings and abuse from their husbands and other men in their families. This woman asked me if I would go to India to teach some of these women how to make jewelry.

I was moved and five days later I flew to Bangalore and sat on a filthy floor for a week teaching these remarkable women how to make jewelry. They were so poor that they typically had only one dress. They lived in dire conditions. Yet, on the last day as I sat with them, one by one they got up and said, "Thank you, Janima [the name they'd given me], thank you so much." I thought I would never stop crying. They were my teachers. They didn't act poor. They didn't act like victims, in spite of the fact that they'd been beaten and abused. They were so open and so appreciative of someone coming to help them. I will never forget them.

If I hadn't listened to my heart and responded to the invitation from that woman on the plane, I would have missed one of the most profound and important moments of my life. So listen to your heart and follow its guidance, even if it doesn't make any sense to the men in your life, because as women, one of our unique and special gifts is being connected to our hearts.

If you feel that inspiration come, don't miss it, because *you* are the one who will receive the greatest gift. Allow yourself to find your song, to discover what you are being guided to share with others.

Know that you are powerful, that there isn't another you on the planet. Get crystal clear about what you want to create in life—not just the things you feel passionate about but things that people compliment you on that you do naturally and have fun doing.

As we said in *The Passion Test*, "What you love and God's will for you are one and the same." It's no accident that you love what you love. By following your heart you will create your own best world. Your passions are the pipelines to your soul.

Get a very clear understanding of what you care about most, what you really feel moved to do, and then strike like lightning in all directions. You have to take decisive action and walk through the doors that start opening. Do everything you can to take the things you want to do to a level of greatness. And then surrender. When you've done everything you can do, relax. Let go. That is when people start to show up to support you and things fall into place so you can do what you are meant to do.

Robyn Benincasa is a world-class endurance athlete, an entrepreneur, and a firefighter. As an adventure racer, she has biked through jungles in Borneo, climbed mountains in Nepal, trekked across lava fields in Fiji, rafted rapids in Chile, and won multiple world championship titles along the way. She is a former Ironman Triathlon competitor, gymnast, diver, cross-country runner, and national champion in judo. Following two total hip replacements, she switched to endurance kayaking and paddled her way into the *Guinness Book of World Records.*

Robyn holds a marketing degree from Arizona State University and maintains a full-time job as a firefighter for the city of San Diego in the nation's first all-women crew. She is the founder of World Class Teams (a team-building program), Flashover Seminars, and the nonprofit Athena Foundation and is a frequent motivational speaker on leadership and teamwork.

Robyn has been featured on NBC, ABC, CNN, ESPN, USA Network, Discovery Channel, Outdoor Life Network, PBS, and Fox News and has been written about in *Fast Company*, *Sports Illustrated*, *Vogue*, *Corporate & Incentive Travel*, the *New York Times*, *Outside*, and *Harper's Bazaar.*

To me, being a woman in any male-dominated arena is an opportunity. If you are an exceptional candidate, if you have the ability and the background and preparation, I think it is a benefit to be a woman because it really makes you stand out from the crowd. It has been my experience that exceptional women stand out, earn respect from their peers, and move up quickly.

The biggest challenge is overcoming assumptions. People think that because you are the girl on the team or the crew you're going to be the weak link, so we have to be at least as good as our male counterparts. I love having the opportunity to surprise people pleasantly.

But just because you're a woman doesn't mean you're always at a physical disadvantage. I think that in endurance racing being a girl is a benefit. Our extra layer of body fat is a huge benefit because of the additional energy stored in it. In the beginning of a race, men are stronger, but toward the end I am stronger than the men. So we *are* different and face somewhat different challenges, but in the end it all balances out.

We have behavioral differences, too, and one of the most important things I have learned about competing or working with men is to be who I am, no matter what. The last thing I want to do is try to act manly around a group of men. In my experience, guys don't want you to be manlier. You'll go further as an accomplished woman than you will by acting as if you want to be a man. As long as you can do the job and hold your own, there is no reason not to be the woman you are—to be that well-organized, fun person the guys want to be around. The engineer on my firefighting crew, Melissa, is a girly girl; until I met her, I was always the tomboy hanging out with the boys. I've worked with Melissa for nine years. I get to witness who she is and how she treats people every day. From her, I've learned how to be a girl's girl and to express my qualities as a woman.

Also, not all the ways in which men treat women differently are negative. In adventure racing, it was nice being a girl because the men were looking out for me in a way. In these races, it was a rule that every team had to have a woman. As I said, in the last round of the race I was usually as strong as the guys. I would never have discovered how awesome women are at endurance had I not competed in those races. In the beginning, the guys would be kind of looking out for me, but toward the end, I was stronger than they were. That actually elevates the team. So I think having a girl on the team builds real synergy and makes everybody better team players.

I see differences between the sexes in my job as a firefighter, too, in situations where huge amounts of brute strength are required. I'm on an all-female crew and we are honest about what we can and cannot do. Yet we absolutely can do our jobs well. My engineer, who drives the engine, is five feet eight and 140 pounds. She has been a firefighter for twenty-two years, and she is one of the few people I know who has pulled people out of a burning building. The point is that it isn't about who can do the most push-ups, but that everybody gives everything they've got. I try to bring that mutual respect to my job and let folks know that it's all about strategy, working together, and solving problems, which requires everybody's experience, skill, and strength.

I'm not sure where my drive to succeed comes from, but I really think "drive" has a genetic component. I have that innate drive mixed with competitiveness. It's not the kind of competitiveness where I absolutely have to beat the other guy—I just want to be the very best *I* can be in my chosen endeavor. Part of that is understanding my special strengths and capitalizing on them. In adventure racing, I was always one of the best paddlers among the women and was even better than a lot of the men. So when I got out of adventure racing, it made sense to go into paddling. You have to know yourself and know your own strengths and make the best of them.

One of my special strengths as a woman is taking care of details and strategic thinking. This is something that girls are really good at. As an adventure racer, I was the team's businessperson and chief strategist. The men were better mountain bikers, but I had these other uniquely feminine strengths to offer the team. As a firefighter, well, half the population is female and 80 percent of our runs are medical aid calls to help women. Women who have just been in an accident or had a miscarriage are very happy to see that the firefighter who comes to their aid is another woman. I think the guys have now come to rely on us to connect with the person who is being rescued. That is often my role. I think women are a bit stronger when it comes to taking care of the human being—beyond the basic process of the medical aid call. The guys tend to go about their business while the girls are more focused on taking care of the person, especially when the person is a woman having female issues.

That human connection is important. It's not just about knocking down walls and putting out fires and cutting into cars. Our all-female crew is very caring for the people and even the animals we rescue. We once ran a call on an older lady, and for some reason she and I just connected. She reminded me very much of my grandmother, and we developed an intense connection almost immediately. We got her to the hospital, and as they were wheeling her into the room, she let go of my hand and said, "I love you." I said, "I love you, too," and we both really meant it. In that short period of time, there was this incredible human connection. I did love that lady, and I will never forget her.

Many of the women in my crew devote time to talking with younger women who are interested in becoming firefighters. I think we have a duty to do that—to tell them about the job and what it requires. There's a sisterhood in our crew, and we share that with women who are thinking about joining our profession. One bit of advice I share relates to the "cavemen" among our colleagues who don't respect the women they work with. We have this unspoken sense that we should just ignore those guys and focus on the really cool people around us. No matter what negativity you hear, remember that it's just a handful of people who are that way. Focus on the positive people, the ones who care for you and want you to succeed.

And of course, I always come back to this: Whatever your goal and no matter how lofty it is, always be yourself. Trying to be someone else brings failure because you *can't* be anyone else. I always told myself that I would approach the job of firefighter by trying to be like a man. Be a girl! Being a female has its own power—especially an accomplished, fun, kind, giving female who is rocking it! That is how you get the most respect and how you get to the next level. It's being who you are and kicking butt and never trying to fit in with the group by being someone you are not.

Also, don't worry too much about your weaknesses, but play to your strengths. Don't be narcissistic, but do analyze yourself. For example, I tried hard for years to be a runner, but I never was a good one. I weigh 150 pounds, and I don't have a runner's genetics, but I beat the crap out of myself for a very long time trying to be a runner. As soon as I turned to paddling, for which I have an inherent ability, I was in front of the race. And not just ahead of the other women—I was in front of the entire race. I'm talking about a 340-mile downriver race called the Missouri River 340. The first time I entered it, I finished second out of 110 solo boats. When something comes more easily to you than to most people and it's something that you love, you've found something precious, one of the strongest aspects of who you are. Of course you have to work at training and developing your talent, but your ability to get to the next level lies in what you love and what you are great at.

I think too many people choose careers for the wrong reasons—status or money or someone else's expectations. If it isn't something that you are a natural at, something that you are great at, something that you are drawn to, then why should you do it? Because your mother wanted you to? Don't get stuck going down the wrong road, someone else's road. Instead, mine the little vein of gold that you find in yourself. That's the most important thing.

Rebecca Blanton is executive director of the California Commission on the Status of Women and Girls. She's pursuing a PhD (ABD) in political science with an emphasis in political psychology from the Graduate Center, City University of New York. She has a BA in psychology from the University of California–Davis. Rebecca has worked as a nonpartisan researcher for the California Research Bureau, where she wrote extensively about the needs of California's women veterans, charter school oversight, and criminal justice issues. Her publications include "California's Women Veterans: Responses to the 2011 Survey" and "California Charter Oversight: Key Elements and Costs." Other professional highlights include teaching at John Jay College in New York City for six years and working for the California Department of Corrections and Rehabilitation.

In politics and policy making, it's critical to have both sexes at the table because we experience the world differently and see it differently, too.

It's a matter of living your gender. As hard as man might try to understand a woman's perspective, there are going to be some things he just won't entirely grasp because he doesn't live the life a woman does. That is why it is so important that both men and women have seats at the table. Because of their different "gender lenses," they have different perspectives on how policy will affect them or their constituencies.

It's also important to recognize that women behave differently in the workplace and pursue their careers differently. I think women tend more than men to delegate and work collaboratively. Men tend to see this as shifting responsibility, while women see it as building community. So sometimes we need to promote the team and promote the collaborative work that women do so well together. On the other hand, I think men are more comfortable claiming credit for their individual accomplishments. As a woman, I try to strike a balance between saying, "This is who I am and what I have accomplished," and promoting the accomplishments of my group or organization. We have to learn to speak up for our personal accomplishments because when our performance is evaluated at the end of the year, men too often see us as less competent, even if our achievements are equal to those of men in the same position.

I think I emphasize the social aspects of the workplace a bit more than my male colleagues. I have happy-hour groups, and I reach out to social networks. Personal relationships are my way of navigating the workplace. We women need to value social networks and understand how they work.

One of the benefits of women's tendency to work more communally or socially is the way in which they often help each other by promoting one another's careers and by mentoring. So much of what I do is driven by who I know and who can recommend me. I know that several jobs I have gotten were based more on who I knew than on my particular skill set.

I've benefitted greatly in my career from mentorship, from meeting people who were willing to help me, and from being open to new experiences. I started my career determined to become a geneticist. Obviously, I ended up on a very different path, and that was the result of being open to people who told me that I was good at something and that I should work for them.

For instance, Chris Wagaman, a Sacramento politician who has worked in the California State Assembly for the last eight years, played a pivotal role in getting me my current position as Executive Director of the California Commission on the Status of Women and Girls. She saw something in me and convinced me to apply for the position. Having somebody a little older and wiser who knew the political scene tell me I had what it takes gave me the confidence I needed and made a huge difference in my career.

Of course, all of us who have been helped by other women need to pay that forward. I've seen hundreds of women working in politics who have tried to raise flags for women's issues. This includes the commissioners I have worked with. And we need to pay it forward on a personal level, too. There are many opportunities to do that. Just take a young woman out to lunch and answer questions about your career. Sponsor an internship. Find ways to use your position to help bring women up—as a boss, as a mentor or an intern director, or just by talking to women and passing on the best piece of career advice you have received. Just be willing to talk about your career— the mistakes you made and what you did right.

It is a great honor to have the job I do with the California Commission for Women and Girls because it gives me a tremendous way to pass on what other women have given to me. So many women before me have worked hard to create opportunities in business and education, and now I have this great opportunity to give back.

Kim Castle, creator of kimTV and star of the reality series *naked kim*, is a fresh voice for today's new breed of feminine leadership. As an overdriving, type-A woman, Kim drove herself to the ground running her business and helping others with theirs. As a result, all the relationships in her life suffered—family, friends, and, most important, the one with herself.

She has worked with large brands, including IBM, DIRECTV, General Motors, Domino's, Wolfgang Puck, Pedigree, Higher Octave Music, Hollywood Celebrity Diet, M&M's, Disney Interactive, Paramount, and many others. She has also guided hundreds of small-business owners in creating their brands—from idea to the Inc. 500 list.

As cocreator of BrandU® and host of various shows, she has co-led a dynamic enterprise that is devoted to empowering entrepreneurs around the world. She has had an impact on more than 30,000 members internationally. Kim has been featured on *CNN Headline News*, *Fox Business News*, Yahoo! Small Business, and *Inc.* magazine. Her work has won a Webby Award for General Motors and she was nominated for the *Los Angeles Business Journal*'s Women Making a Difference Award.

Funny, fashionable, vivacious, and vulnerable, she shows powerhouse women (and the extraordinary men who love them) that in order to take care of their world, they must take care of themselves first. Learn more about her shows at KimCastle.com.

I've never understood what people mean when they say, "It is not personal, it is business." That's because I don't separate who I am as a person from my business; I make everything personal first and foremost. I am more about the relationships and connecting with people first. And sometimes that means that things slow down because I would much rather make relationships and get that kind of energy going.

Men and women do a lot of things differently, including the way they process information. When working together, it's important to recognize these differences to minimize miscommunication and to work effectively. Men are typically linear thinkers, which means they process information in a very straightforward "point A to point B," step-by-step way. Women, on the other hand, are nonlinear thinkers. Our thought processes are characterized by expansion in multiple directions and diffuse awareness, rather than moving in a single direction. What's more, men are wired to discuss what they think as opposed to what they feel, just the opposite of women.

So what's the problem? Nothing really—*if* you recognize and embrace these differences. The business of business itself is very male-centric and linear in focus: You have an idea, you create and sprinkle in some innovation, you bring it to market, and you rinse and repeat. On the other hand, for women, it's all about creation, with which women are truly connected. Our power of creation is something with which we are born. But the creative process is more unstructured and far-reaching than the linear approach. As a result, there's a "culture clash" between these different styles. As a creative director and digital content creator, my work requires a lot of creativity; I help clients develop and express their brands via digital media and expose them to new audiences. As a nonlinear creator, I personally have to work hard to follow the linear path in order to deliver projects on schedule.

One can view men as typically being "detail" people while women are "big-picture" oriented. I definitely think of myself as a "big-picture" person. When I work with a client, I don't base potential results on their current state; instead, I create a plan based on the client's end goal. To plan strategically from where you are standing today is not going to get you very far.

I believe, in general, that women bring a greater understanding of the whole (again, that big-picture quality). It's how we are wired: multidirectional multitaskers. There's something about the old saying about moms having eyes in the back of their heads. We see and take everything in. When we walk into a room, everything talks to us. The opposite is true of men. Single focus gives a man the ability to walk into a room and walk over a pair of socks to find his phone and not even see the socks.

On the downside, I think that many women put their needs last. We go, go, go, and run until we drop. We rest because we're forced to by running out of steam—we rest just until we get a jump start and we're off again. Unfortunately, it takes far more energy to restore us from empty. It's important to remember that we have a responsibility to ourselves first, and that responsibility is to be whole, happy, and peaceful. In order to take care of the world around us, we must take care of ourselves first. That's the hardest thing to learn. Business, motherhood, and all of those other roles come after.

Women who have taken an idea and made their dreams come true inspire me and encourage me to go that extra mile. Because my life revolves around entertainment and brand, I am certainly inspired by women like Ellen DeGeneres, Oprah, Skinnygirl creator Bethenny Frankel, and Jennifer Lopez. I'm also drawn to amazing lifestyle designers like Tory Burch, Donna Karan, and the late Anita Roddick of The Body Shop. These highly successful women created great wealth and security for themselves and the people in their world by being fueled by an idea and a dream, a willingness to play full out, and a deep commitment to continue until they reached their place of full expression.

But the meaning of "success" is often nebulous for women. There is no hard and fast definition of exactly what success means. It can be fleeting or can remain a constant in a woman's life. And although most people have to work hard to get it, for others, it practically falls into their laps.

I can attribute what I think of as my successes to three things:

The first is *a willingness to keep growing, keep challenging myself, and push past so-called boundaries.* For example, I was a sickly child and suffered from chronic asthma. Because I was severely allergic to trees common in my hometown of Miami, simply breathing could cause an asthma attack. I found that being in the water was a very soothing thing, so I swam a lot and became a synchronized swimmer. At the age of seven or eight, I thought, *What would happen if I stayed underwater for longer period of time? Would that do anything?* After much practice, I found that if I would do underwater laps I could expand my lung capacity; no matter what, I wouldn't stop and I kept doing it and doing it and before I realized it, my asthma was completely gone.

The second factor is my persistence. *When I make my mind up on something, I don't let go until I make it happen.* My husband sometimes calls me relentless or obsessive because when I focus on an idea or something I want to experience or accomplish, I literally won't stop until I get it. I'm not sure where I got it from, but I've been that way for as long as I can remember.

Third and finally, *I am always aware of how I make people feel.* That has always been the wind in my sails. It's my genius and a big part of what I bring to the world. This was a major reason why I branched out on my own to create kimTV. I'm passionate about creating television shows wrapped around an idea and fueled by the values of a brand.

I'm a big believer in honoring one's source, an appreciation of the greater aspect of where something comes from. To "honor the source" means that you acknowledge where you got the knowledge, and use that knowledge to help someone else. By doing so, you honor the hand in front of you, to whom you're giving the information, and you honor the person behind or beside you who gave you that information. In the process, you create and then maintain a connection —reaching, handing, reaching, handing. It's an active demonstration of context that surrounds us. This creates a circle of strong, intelligent women, and provides a connection and a place where we foster each other.

Whether we realize it or not, the world looks to us for peace, flow, beauty—a state of "rightness." It's our role to create it, through our work, through our family, through our communities...but first we have to be it for ourselves.

Dame DC Cordova, a philanthropist and humanitarian, is known as an ambassador of new education. She is CEO of the Excellerated Business Schools® for Entrepreneurs and Money & You®, a global organization with more than 100,000 graduates worldwide, particularly from the Asian Pacific and North American, and now expanding into the Hispanic, markets. Through these graduates, who include many successful entrepreneurs and today's wealth "gurus," DC's work has touched the lives of millions all over the world. Courses are taught in English and Chinese.

She is the author of the comprehensive systems manual *Money-Making Systems*, and has coauthored many books. DC has participated in more than a dozen motivational films and television shows. She has been interviewed around the world in every type of media, and even hosted the *Money & You* radio show. DC is building a global women's platform called "Women, Cash & Divine Matters." She is working on the first book in support of this platform, which will be translated to several languages to meet the needs of her international audience.

In 2010, DC was knighted by the Sovereign Order of the Orthodox Knights Hospitaller of Saint John of Jerusalem for her lifelong service to humanity. She is a founding member of the Transformational Leadership Council (TLC) and the Southern California Association of Transformational Leaders (ATL), facilitator for the

Pachamama Alliance Symposium, council member of the Women Speakers' Association, promoter of the global campaign "Four Years. Go.," an Asia Pacific development consultant, and a member of the board of advisors of SuperLab, founding faculty member for Compassion Happens, Inc., and international business development advisor for the California Women's Conference. She supports numerous other humanitarian and nonprofit organizations as a mentor and champion—most recently having created the Humanitarian Mastermind, starting in Cancun, Mexico, to educate, guide, and empower humanitarians.

When I began in the education and training field at the age of twenty-nine, I had to conquer some formidable prejudices pertaining to my age, gender, and ethnicity. Some people doubted my abilities because I was too young—and considered "a little dumb" (that's according to them, not me)—and a woman. As a native of Chile, I spoke with an accent, which some people equate with a lack of intelligence. The notion couldn't be further from the truth because, oftentimes, an accent is indicative of a person who speaks multiple languages (I speak three). Interestingly, people's preconceived notions actually played to my favor at times. For instance, because people assumed that I wasn't that smart, they wouldn't negotiate as smartly as they could have. Having learned the art of negotiation as a professional in the legal field for eight years, I could be a savvy negotiator because I was always prepared with facts about the persons involved and the topic in question.

In the 1970s, women were just gaining visibility in business. So I had to study harder, prepare meticulously, and be on my "A" game at all times. Women, in general, have a tendency to be more emotional than men (and there are exceptions). This inherent emotional quotient is quite often not a good match when dealing with men. I had to learn to master my emotions. I'm thankful that, by that time, my mentor began learning about neurolinguistic programming and I learned a tremendous amount about how to master my emotions, so I was able to emulate the people with whom I was working.

That's not to say that my progress followed a straight line. I made mistakes during the learning process. I went through a series of "learning experiences" (mistakes) over several years while I created my own persona by emulating leaders with whom I identified. During the process, I created my own "toolbox" of helpful skills and techniques. For example, despite trying hard, there were moments when my behavior was too aggressive and I offended others. I had not learned yet to be diplomatic in presenting my questions or challenging their points of view. Because I didn't want this to continue to be a problem, I asked for feedback from people around me. I would take people with me to meetings. We would debrief afterward and they gave me feedback about my behavior during those meetings.

I strongly suggest that everyone have some sort of team, a Mastermind group, or mentors who can provide you with feedback. It was the best support that I could have gotten. I've found that building networks of key mentors and friends helps me to receive important feedback and balance my professional life and personal life. Some of my most important mentors have been women. So have my most valuable partners and employees. Women have amazing intuition, the ability to see the big picture, a greater ability to multitask, and are able to be completely focused on more than one project at a time. I've found that the best multitaskers are women who have raised children. Although there are always exceptions, most males tend to focus on one thing at a time and females tend to multitask. When running a business, people who can handle many things at once are essential; women are excellent at that.

A few very special women have made me a wiser, stronger, and better person:

The first is my mother. I come from a line of women who were entrepreneurs. My mother began to train me at a very young age; I didn't have the choice to be anything but successful!

The second is Sondra Ray. She had a tremendous influence on my life. She taught me about global travel and about how to expand my horizons and be open to many different experiences. She also introduced me to Marshall Thurber and Bobbi DePorter, who created the world's first transformational experiential business school, where I discovered my business purpose and learned further distinctions in business to complement the business systems that I had learned in the legal field. Plus, my study in higher consciousness inspired me to leverage myself more effectively. I ended up taking over that business once they moved on to do other work.

The third is Dr. Jannie Chan. As one of Asia's most successful businesswomen, Dr. Chan taught me further distinctions about money, wealth, business, generosity, trust, commitment, and family.

She taught me how to work productively with Asia's top leaders (both men and women) and how to be a good diplomat.

Two other women also taught me very valuable lessons about resilience and bravery:

My friend Rachel Best was a graduate of our programs and a personal assistant of mine in Australia during the mid-1980s. Rachel had surgery for ovarian cancer exactly on 9/11/01—one of America's toughest days. Her prognosis was not good—two to three months to live. But Rachel being Rachel, she lived another *five years*. I spent a solid year with her and I saw her tenacity in researching to educate herself on different treatment options. We would go to Mexico and have alternative treatments together so that she wouldn't feel like she was alone. She moved me tremendously.

After her death, I called her doctor to thank him for all of the wonderful things he had done for her. He thanked me for what Rachel and I had done together. "Three months to live" was the diagnosis in his reality—but not hers. Rachel taught me about strength. When you have someone who beats the odds at that level, it can't help but affect all aspects of your life, personal and professional.

Later, I met my then-boyfriend's mother, Sue, who had stage IV lung cancer. One of the things I learned from Sue was her elegance in confronting the end of her life and doing it in a way that was so graceful. I was able to support her during that time. She was loving and grateful.

Rachel and Sue also reaffirmed something for me that I had learned early on: Life can be tough. Many people are not prepared for the tough parts of life. We all experience challenges like job loss, economic changes, falling in love with the wrong person, or losing people that we love.

I lived in Chile until I was twelve years old. My family moved to Los Angeles, where I grew up as a typical Californian teenager. When I was 18 years old, my first love was killed and I miscarried his baby—a rough way to start adulthood. After that shaky start, it took me many years to come to a place of trust. The one thing that I learned through those rough times in my life was to have a system in place to prepare me if the worst happened. I have a plan A, plan B, plan C, plan D, *and* plan E. It is called having choices. When you feel like you are having the worst time of your life, take three deep breaths and say, "This too shall pass." You'll be centered and you'll begin to identify options to remedy the issue. But you must find at least three to six options. A lot of women forget that our sixth sense, or intuition, is something men would kill for. Give yourself choices and resources and then pick the one that is the best. Just know things are going to happen. Both young and old women friends of mine tend to be shocked when something bad happens. Don't be. Just plan ahead.

Eli Davidson, national expert in the fields of personal and professional re-invention, business expert, executive mentor, international bestselling author, and sought-after thought leader, is recognized as one of America's top coaches. She is a featured columnist with the *Huffington Post*, reaching twenty-one million readers. Her book, *Funky to Fabulous*, is an international best seller and won three national book awards (Independent Publisher, USA Best Books, and the Indie Next Generation Motivational Book of the Year).

Eli's trademarked business growth system was a cover story for *Kiplinger's Personal Finance*. She has appeared on the *Today Show* and *Dr. Phil's Decision House* and NBC, ABC, and Fox TV affiliates. Eli speaks on overcoming obstacles. She gives audiences the Turnaround Techniques[SM]—a system to implement change that she developed and trademarked. A resident of Los Angeles, her advice has been featured in publications as diverse as *Better Homes and Gardens* and the *Los Angeles Business Journal*.

Eli is a graduate of Sarah Lawrence College. She has a master's degree in spiritual psychology from the University of Santa Monica, where she was named Student of the Year.

It is an exciting time to be a woman mentoring women entrepreneurs! My focus is on the service-based industries, which encompass 65 percent of all women's businesses. During 2011 and 2012, the big boys created 87 percent of the capital, while women currently receive only 4 percent of that capital to fund their businesses. So it's my mission to create a million small-business millionaires. Women now have the opportunity to build their businesses and thrive like never before, and it is exhilarating to help other women further their careers and get ahead in business.

Research has shown that we women sense emotion in twenty-three sectors of our brains while men sense emotion in nine sectors of their brains. What exactly does that mean, and do those findings reinforce the old stereotype that women are overly emotional and can't be trusted with strategic business decisions? Far from it. In fact, it's just the opposite. All business is about relationships and women have been in the relationship business for thousands of years. Because women leverage those incredible skills of communication, compassion, and emotional courage, we have so much more depth to offer our clients than our male colleagues.

Women bring to the table intuition, empathy, and compassion. But perhaps even more than that, we collaborate in a more profound way than our male counterparts. Women can encourage a level of compassion and emotional courage that men are not equipped to provide. As a woman leader, I am far more intuitive than my male counterparts, allowing me to see and seize market opportunities much faster than men can. Men often will want to get the data, perform research, and do a market study, and then re-analyze the data and put it through committee. Women, on the other hand, rely on their intuition and often go with it. So my behavior means that I can create new programs and execute them faster than my male counterparts because I don't have to filter information through the sieve of market analysis.

Business is about being nimble and recognizing opportunities quickly; that intuitive edge has allowed me to take advantage of opportunities that men probably never considered. For example, I taught myself how to write, wrote a book, and won three national book awards. And then, even though I was told it was impossible, I got myself on all of the national television shows, like the *Today Show*, without a publicist. I think those are intuitive risks and goals that a man might never attempt because the odds against those things happening were five million to one. So I think as women, we do have access to a deeper knowing more quickly than men.

With that said, women face a variety of challenges—chief among them is the fact that we must still "prove ourselves" in a way that men don't. A study performed by the Catalyst Organization monitored women globally; what they saw was that a woman who was too meek or nice was considered a second-rate employee or business owner and a woman who was assertive was a bitch.

First and foremost, women must be confident in and recognize their value. I think of it this way—a diamond is the most condensed form of wealth in the world. Inside of us is that condensed form of value. Recognize that value and use it to solve your clients' urgent, pervasive, and expensive problems. You're then positioned to leverage your time to create efficiently and build your business, generating the income so that you can give back and be an influence on our world.

You can refine the quality of your diamond by:

- Dedicating yourself to a mission that is much bigger than you. This is a process of identifying and clarifying the profound value you offer as a woman (i.e., your soul and spirit) and translating that into how you can serve others.
- Identifying how to generate income to establish a financial foundation. We can't change the world unless we make some serious money.
- Giving back.

A crucial element in a woman's blueprint to success is paying it forward. It is urgent and essential that we, as women, mentor other women. I have mentoring students that I take on. One of the things that they see is that men have a much more developed network of mentorship than women do. So find a mentor and be a mentor. Alert women to the support we have, which many women don't even know about. For instance, Dell has a $100 million investment fund targeted to women in business. One way I am paying it forward is by letting women know about this fund and a variety of other resources. By owning your value and standing in your true identity, your influence can make a distinct, positive difference in the world.

Julia Dilts is the CEO and co-founder of Maverick angels, an angel investment network based in Southern California with affiliate chapters in Western Europe and Tel Aviv, which she founded with her late husband, John Dilts. Maverick Angels focuses on mentoring and training global entrepreneurs to fund promising early-stage companies resulting in successful and self-sustaining businesses.

Additionally, Maverick is presently creating strong affiliations with other angel groups, universities, incubators, accelerators, and government agencies to train, mentor, and coach aspiring entrepreneurs via their "Maverick Angels Investment Accelerator for Entrepreneurs" seminar. This monthly course is based on studying capitalized start-ups from around the world over a ten-year period to determine what success factors an entrepreneur must possess to become attractive to investors. Additionally, they have also enrolled experts in debt/equity financing, valuations and corporate structuring, legal counsel, and social media to guest lecture at their Investment Accelerator seminar.

Before Julia's work with Maverick Angels, she was the co-owner of Dilts Ventures, a corporate management consulting firm with an entrepreneurial approach to business. Julia and John advised corporate giants such as Nestlé USA, Pratt & Whitney Rocketdyne, Fiat, and Kraft Foods in areas such as entrepreneurial training within the corporate culture, innovative approaches to product development and market-entry strategies, and visionary leadership.

Today, while I was working from my home office, I saw a hummingbird perched on a branch for an extraordinarily long time. My immediate thought was that I had so much work to do, I couldn't keep staring at the pretty bird outside of my window. But instead of writing another e-mail, I watched this beautiful, delicate creature. It reminded me that I had just been given an incredible gift, and of a valuable lesson.

Life steers us into some very interesting turns. If someone told me more that a decade ago that I would be championing entrepreneurs and stepping in as the CEO of my own investment group, I would never have believed them. I thought of myself as a creative, a crazy woman on Instagram. I have a butterfly tattoo . . . How in the world did I end up in finance and in the international world of entrepreneurship? The answer: a man.

I first met John when we were both attending UCLA in the 1980s. There I was with my big hair and my pearly pink lipstick while John was sporting Ray-Bans and preppy button-down shirts. John became a senior political staff writer for *The Daily Bruin*, our college newspaper; I was the copy editor who would edit all of his articles. In fact, I honestly fell in love with his writing before I fell in love with him because he and I first met face to face months after I prepared his articles for print. The whole reason I went to UCLA was to become a journalist. Even at a young age, I knew that I wanted to write and express myself to educate and engage people. I was longing for a creative outlet, and that's what John and I had in common as we began our courtship.

We were in school during the Reagan years. Life was big and bold, and women wore power suits. My confidence levels shot through the roof during my college years. I had my life all planned out: marry the adoring husband, take on a fast-track career, have a family, buy a house—a road map to happiness. What I didn't factor into my perfect little formula was that life has its own plans in mind for each of us.

Seven years ago, my husband, John Dilts, and I founded Maverick Angels. Our vision was to create a robust angel group, which included an entrepreneurial training course, now titled the "Investment Accelerator," to help start-up companies perfect their pitches and increase their chances of becoming successfully funded. John and I complemented each other as a team—building our angel network and seeking out the best and brightest entrepreneurs to present to our investors.

Around the time that John and I founded Maverick Angels, John and his brother Robert, a well-known behavioral scientist, were involved in a ten-year study interviewing more than three hundred capitalized entrepreneurs from around the world. The game-changing findings from this study became the genesis of our Investment Accelerator.

Have you ever wondered why one person will achieve success while another who started up the same type of business has to close up shop? When you take a closer look, the people who achieve success are more likely to be more open-minded, be coachable, have enrolled mentors, have a clear vision of where they are taking their company, and initiate can-do attitudes when facing challenges. "Reframing" the tough times into opportunities is also an essential behavioral strategy that successful people will likely use.

The study revealed that there are eight Success Factors, or personality traits of entrepreneurs that contribute to their business success. Support System. Motivated. Inspired. Fearless. Charitable. Confident. Coachable. Team player. If you are an entrepreneur and your DNA includes these eight Success Factors, it is proven that investors will be more likely to write you checks. These behaviors, along with knowing your venture and financials cold, are the road map to entrepreneurial success.

Fast-forward to August 2, 2010. John passed away from cancer a week after he was diagnosed, and my world would never be the same. There I was—suddenly a grieving widow holding on to our beloved angel group, John's legacy. From the Dilts brothers' study, I learned that true leaders strive to create something bigger than themselves. This motivated me to keep the Maverick vision alive as I stepped into provide immediate leadership just days after John passed. As anyone can imagine, it was the greatest challenge of my life—and I found the eight Success Factors guiding me.

During difficult times, I rely on what motivates and inspires me in order to keep moving in a positive direction. I draw on the strength that others and the memory of John provide to me. Interestingly enough, a supportive spouse or someone close to you is the number one Success Factor in the entrepreneurial study. If you have a go-to partner or posse to cheer you on, the odds are in your favor that you will drive a thriving business.

The entrepreneurs who have the chips stacked against them often have a closed-minded way of doing business, which isolates them from their team and alienates those who are willing to offer guidance. Eventually, many of these leaders close down their operations due to their myopic belief systems. I would guess that these entrepreneurs were not motivated to create a vision for themselves, their teams, and potential investors, and weren't willing to be resourceful and flexible in order to turn roadblocks into strategic wins for their companies.

My hat goes off, though, to those entrepreneurs who have tried fiercely and, for whatever reasons, had to shut their doors. I have great respect for those individuals. To them I say, "Be proud of your battle scars and turn them into a badge of honor. Please, give it another go!"

No matter how Webster's defines entrepreneurship, it does not describe the grit it takes to be an entrepreneur. Although the media tends to cast a shiny spotlight on those who have achieved great success, there is rarely a mention of the entrepreneurs quietly working endless hours, enduring great sacrifice, and living a more modest lifestyle in order to pursue their dreams. These unsung heroes and heroines especially are my greatest role models.

The best part of my position at Maverick Angels is connecting with these entrepreneurs. I am fascinated by their passion, their war stories, and what motivates them to keep going. I also draw encouragement by remembering those enterprising men and women who lived before us and faced incredible challenges to make the world better for the following generations. We may not have had many of today's technologies, freedoms, and legal rights if these individuals had not been brave and fearless.

Going through my husband's passing has made me somewhat fearless—and this inspires me. My mantra to be fearless in business comes down to this question: What is the worst that can happen? Most likely, you will not end up living on the street and going hungry. If you are well prepared, plan ahead for life's curve balls, and are confident that you will always land on your feet, then you are well on your way to the path of success.

Along with being brave and fearless, our entrepreneurial ancestors have also proven it is essential to feel worthy to grab the brass ring—to feel confident. I practice this behavior daily, and it helps me turn limiting thoughts into plans of action. Entrepreneurs must believe in their visionary powers and innovative minds. In the study, we discovered that entrepreneurs must give themselves permission to become successful, not self-sabotage that success.

I also find inspiration by giving back—by coaching entrepreneurs, volunteering my time, and making contributions to benefit entrepreneurial causes. Showing compassion toward others is another Success Factor among star-quality entrepreneurs. Whenever I attend Maverick's monthly seminar and see how the behavioral and business models motivate promising start-ups to think big and sharpen their pitches, it validates why I champion entrepreneurs—the pioneers of our day.

Clearly, a positive attitude, loads of passion, and tribal leadership to help entrepreneurs march forward are all key to success. Anyone who ever said that being an entrepreneur was easy has never been an entrepreneur! When times are good, life is great. However, . times are tough and morale is low, entrepreneurs must draw from the eight Success Factors to motivate themselves and their teams to believe that tomorrow is a new day filled with opportunities.

Despite the setbacks and challenges entrepreneurs currently face, the good news is that start-up companies are growing at record numbers globally. It amazes me that so many are willing to give up that comfy corporate paycheck for a life of unpredictability and risk in the name of success. Yet during times of economic challenge, opportunities for innovation, prosperity, and start-up companies abound. Now is the time to become an aspiring entrepreneur if you are searching for more than what the status quo has to offer.

In my life, I have had a lion's share of hard knocks, trials and tribulations, and sweet victories, which I feel honored to share with you here. My wish is that my story will in some small way help you through the challenging times and inspire you on your entrepreneurial journey.

Gloria Feldt is the definition of a twenty-first-century Renaissance woman. Called a "feminist icon" by Amazon.com, she is a nationally recognized social and political advocate for women's rights, and an author, an educator, an executive, and the co-founder and president of Take the Lead, a non-profit organization with a goal to propel women to leadership parity in politics, business, and their personal lives by 2025.

With thirty years of CEO experience, she served as president of Planned Parenthood Federation of America from 1996 to 2005. She is the *New York Times* bestselling author of *No Excuses: Nine Ways Women Can Change How We Think About Power*, as well as three other books. Her commentary has appeared in the *New York Times*, *USA Today*, the *Wall Street Journal*, and the *Washington Post*, among other publications.

Gloria was named to *Vanity Fair*'s "Top 200 Women, Legends, Leaders, and Trailblazers." She currently teaches "Women, Power, and Leadership" at Arizona State University.

The nineteenth-century abolitionist and women's rights crusader Sojourner Truth stated, "If women want more power than they've got, why don't they just take it and not just be talking about it?" Her words exemplify an attitude that has guided and inspired me as a CEO, as a women's advocate, and as a person. If we, as women, want something more than what we have, we can't just whine about it, we must go and do it!

And do it we have. In the United States, we've made great strides in advancing new inclusive legislation and removed many of the barriers that have denied women equality and access to leadership roles. But we're not completely there yet.

For several decades now, it's been my mission to see women get equal treatment under the law, at work, and in society as a whole. Through the nonprofit organization Take the Lead, which my colleague Amy Litzenberger and I founded, I share my experience so that we might reach the goal of women coming to full personhood and enjoying equality in our society. Specifically, our mission is to prepare, develop, inspire, and propel women to take their fair and equal share of leadership positions across all sectors by 2025.

Although we have removed many of the barriers to women's equality and leadership roles, there is still more to do. There are many books and articles that tell women how they need to change *themselves* when, in fact, it's the *system* that needs to be changed. We need to learn how to change the system for the benefit of our daughters and granddaughters so that it will be more supportive and welcoming and so that it will strengthen the power of women to be more confident and comfortable contributing their intelligence, skills, and capabilities to society.

However, the main challenge we have now is primarily within ourselves. We hang on to habits learned back in the days when our power and opportunities were limited, and these old habits prevent

49

us from asking for promotions or asking for a raise, putting ourselves forward, and seeing ourselves as political candidates or the heads of corporations. That's what my work focuses on now. I believe that the work that I do helps women to embrace the power they own and understand its dynamics.

I look at this as an exciting opportunity to address power-related issues—for instance, we know women are socialized to negotiate better for others than for themselves. It's important for women to realize that when they effectively address their own professional and financial needs, it makes things better for other women too.

I grew up in a time when women were powerless over their own finances, their options for employment, and their own bodies. I married young, and by the age of twenty had three children. I couldn't even open up my own credit card account without my husband's approval. "The Pill" didn't exist and abortions were illegal. Although I wanted to become a high school teacher, it took me twelve years to finish college in order to qualify. Then I was offered a job at a small Planned Parenthood affiliate in my native Texas. Over time, I rose through the ranks of the organization, reaching the position of President and CEO of the Planned Parenthood Federation of America. As the CEO of a large national nonprofit organization, I used all of the skills that the CEOs of GE or Ford Motor Company would use—but without the resources that they have (which I think is a fairly typical thing for women).

Was everything in my life perfect? No. But I was able to use the power that I had to build dedicated teams of bright and talented individuals intent on getting the job done. It's been my philosophy to take what I have and make something good out of it. I'm a positive person and always believe that anything is possible. I fervently believe that when women share equally in power and leadership, the world will be a better place for everyone. And that is why my personal mission today is to encourage, teach, and inspire women to take their fair and equal share of leadership roles in all aspects of life, from the boardroom to the bedroom.

Marion Freijsen is cofounder and chief operating officer of EFactor Group Corp., the publicly traded parent of, among others, a global social network for entrepreneurs, providing them with online and offline support regarding funding, business development, and cost savings and knowledge. Marion built the EFactor network to include more than 1,000,000 members in five years, and EFactor currently has approximately 700,000 members in the US and provides 100 events annually globally. Marion is also the owner of Elegio BV, a Dutch company providing business consulting and management expertise in the areas of strategy, vision, finance, international expansion, and business development for clients such as ING, Lloyds, BASF, and Numico. In addition, Marion was the founder and the former CEO and executive board member of OHM Inc., a sales consulting firm serving emerging technology companies. Marion launched OHM with no outside investment, and in five years she and her cofounders established a portfolio of more than 100 clients. Her expertise includes arranging meetings for clients with senior management and/or board members of Fortune 1500 companies, such as HSBC, Barclays Bank, ING, BP, Shell, and Exxon-Mobil. Marion's background also includes serving as a former vice president (Central Europe) for Currenex Ltd., Commercial Director of Speedport NV, Country Manager (Benelux) for Newsedge Corp., Major Account Manager for ICV Ltd. / S&P Comstock, and Account Manager for Bloomberg Financial Markets.

She is a frequent guest on TV networks such as NBC, CBS, ABC, and *Wall Street Journal* TV, and has sat on committees of both the Dutch and US governments on job creation and funding innovation.

Marion coauthored *The N-Factor: How Networking Can Change the Dynamics of Your Business* in 2007 with EFactor cofounder Adrie Reinders. Her newest book, *The EFactor: Entrepreneurship in the Social Media Age*, was released in 2012.

Marion holds a degree in international sales and marketing from the Chartered Institute of Marketing, UK.

I looked at the man in total amazement. He stood there calmly in the middle of his elaborate house in Ras-al-Hamra, Oman, dressed in his dishdasha, with a brightly colored keffiyeh on his head and, to top it off, modern Ray-Ban sunglasses. He wasn't too bad-looking, I pondered, but still—his proposal to my then-husband would have sounded rather preposterous to any European, let alone someone like me: twenty years old, born and raised in the especially progressive Netherlands. He had just—his voice was still ringing in my ears—offered my soon-to-be ex-husband ten racing camels and a fair amount of cash . . . for me! And I could tell by the way he was looking at my husband that he was dead serious! He sincerely hoped to add a young, blonde, blue-eyed woman to his harem—that was very clear. I wasn't really too sure my husband wasn't tempted.

Luckily for me, it remains one of those many anecdotes that make up a lifetime of experiences and not one that came to fruition—my husband very politely declined the offer and whisked me home to our not-half-as-ornate-and-exotic house in the European zone of the city. It gave me a great insight, however, early on in my life, about a woman's value in a man's world. That wasn't just because this was the Middle East, where one might expect to see strong divisions between male and female roles (but where I often found women to be the ones wearing the pants at home!). Everywhere in the world, to varying degrees and with varying amounts of subtlety, women aren't seen as the people with whom you do business—men are. Men may use their skills and knowledge to gain and use financial resources (as in bartering for a new harem member); women *are* those resources— or at least we are not expected to deal in those resources the same way men do. In other words, women aren't seen as camel owners. Without wanting to traipse out stereotypes, everywhere in the world, women often take the supportive role automatically and leave it to the guys to beat their chests and fight the war. In my mind, even that early in adulthood, I intuitively felt that it need not be that way.

I remember very clearly a camping trip, when I was about fourteen, with the Girl Scout troop of which I was an enthusiastic supporter. It was one of those summer camp things where a group of young girls lies awake all night giggling and telling each other stories (without the ill effects of no sleep one tends to suffer at a much later age, alas. . .). We talked and talked and inevitably we hit upon the subject of "when I grow up . . . ." My friends all dreamt up the more traditional picture: husband, wealth, babies—usually in that order. I listened to all of them and kept thinking to myself with some curiosity, *Why do you need a husband to be rich? I'll become a millionaire all by myself!*

I have always been an adventurer at heart. I grew up in a rather run-of-the-mill family, where my parents taught me early on that independence was a good thing and made my siblings and me rely on our own imaginations to solve problems and issues. I am glad they did—it has helped me tremendously along the way. There was no "I can't do that" in our family; my dad was hugely creative and always keen to figure out how to do things himself, from making typical handicrafts for our home to attempting to make his own shoes (at which he luckily failed. I think my mother would have cringed to go anywhere with him wearing his own fabrications as much as we cringed at having to wear her homemade clothes!). So I guess thoughts of a glass ceiling or the impossibility of millionaire dreams were beyond me. I just didn't understand why they would even *be* impossible—and from an early age, I set out to make my own dreams come true rather than relying on others (however much I loved them) to make them come true for me.

I left my home country a rather naive twenty-year-old to go live in the Middle East for a number of years. It was the start of a long tour abroad for me (in the end, taking more than eighteen years to settle back in my own country again . . . for a little while at least). After leaving the Middle East, I went to live in the United Kingdom on my own. I wasn't ready yet to go back to the Netherlands and felt that I could be close to my home country without giving up my traveling days quite yet. I had developed a taste for experiencing different cultures—although I did make the mistake of thinking the English culture would be easier and more closely related to my Dutch heritage than the Middle Eastern one was! Starting as a secretary at a merchant bank, it didn't take very long before I became a credit analyst in managed and leveraged buy-outs for the bank. I was lucky to a degree, of course; my boss then really gave me all the opportunity I could have hoped for. At that time, finance was still very much a man's game. But my boss and mentor, Mr. Hietink, was unusual and really gave equal opportunity to those who wanted to take it. From where I am sitting now, with those years in mind, I believe that "equal opportunity" is not just a right, actually… it is also a duty—and not just on the side of the person granting it. You don't just "get" an opportunity anywhere or anytime you want it. You have to work for it, you have to show you want it, and you also have to continue to live up to the promise you make when it has been granted to you.

Mr. Hietink much later told me a story that resonates deeply with me. He called it "the tennis players versus the soccer players." A traditional workplace is made up of a bunch of soccer players. They all play the same game; they know the rules intuitively, and they understand the strategies behind it and the tactics involved. All of a sudden, a tennis player comes along who wants to join in…and that creates an interesting scenario. Either the tennis player adapts and slowly learns the game of soccer until she can play the same game, the soccer players give up a little bit of their soccer game and see that the game of tennis has some interesting new aspects that can make the overall game they play better and stronger, or the tennis player gives up and leaves the soccer fans to it, with neither party having learned anything new and each returning to their own games, exclaiming how much they loathe the other game and all it entails.

In my mind, the only real option is the middle one: being open-minded and taking every opportunity that comes your way to learn something new. If you continue adding what you learn to your own repertoire, the game—whatever that game may be—becomes richer and more interesting and infinitely more fun!

This is where a glass ceiling ceases to exist. As a woman, you have a lot of wonderful skills to add to the game the men like to play. It isn't just that you have to adapt and play by their rules...though it's never bad to learn something new. You can equally, patiently set out to change their game and make them adapt a little to play yours. Of course, there will be a number of guys who never learn. They don't *want* to learn and will always fight whatever you bring to the table. But I know you; you can find a way around that. You are by definition more creative than someone whose mind is so closed that he cannot even see there may be different ways of doing things.

Much has changed in the world of finance since I first started there. It was definitely a challenge to "grow up" in that environment. Even little things became huge—like overturning an unspoken policy that women could only wear skirts to a client meeting (seriously?!). The bank was really quite adamant, but over time, I won that battle and started showing up in sharp-looking trouser suits. To me, it was worth fighting for; in dictating how I could dress, the management was holding women in a different category than men. Can you imagine telling a guy what to wear to work? I learned during those years that humor was really the key to crafting change. Being aggressive or always wanting to fight every little detail wouldn't have gotten me anywhere at all—but humor is such a great tool. If someone mistook me, as the only woman in the room, for the typist and asked me to take notes, I would smile and say, "Of course," then hand them my card (with my title) and ask them if they didn't mind "being Mum, and pouring the tea" for the group. I have seen many guys blush and falter once they realized their mistake—which only worked in my favor. They always remembered me and treated me with deference from then on. I didn't make them look foolish, and I hardly ever aggressively attempted to make my point; it was all a matter of timing and persistence. The great thing about being the only woman in many of these meetings is that *everyone* is more likely to remember you. You stand out, and that is such a huge advantage. If it comes to new opportunities, you can simply pick up the phone and introduce yourself as "that woman at the last meeting"...whereas the guys all looked the same! Yes, of course it has its downsides, too. You learn to deal with the passes, the little digs, and so on. It's par for the course, but as long as you have the inner confidence to feel you don't have to engage on that level nor play along just to be liked, you get to go a long, long way. And you will be respected by your male counterparts for it.

A "long way" for me eventually led to taking a year out from my career. I got so, so tired of working my behind off for companies that I decided literally to pack my (bicycle) bags and go. I had a whole year off, cycling around the world. From South America to New Zealand and Australia and eventually from Spain across the Pyrenees and the Alps to Italy, it was bliss—totally different from my twenty years spent building a career in finance and technology. My only thoughts in the morning were, *Where shall I sleep at night?* and *What shall I eat?* instead of the usual list of things I'd been waking up with in the morning related to work and career and the household and so on. Simple—cycle till you drop, set up camp, and have food. Sleep and then do it all over again...for a whole year.

For me, the year out was a way to rethink what I wanted out of my career and my life. When you are young, you focus on the next steps in your career: a better job, more money, higher status, a bigger car. But sometimes a pause is what's needed to rediscover why you are moving in a certain direction and evaluate whether that direction is helping you grow and develop into a better you. My year out made me refocus on the things that were important to me and then apply those things when eventually I did settle into work again. It gave me time to take my old "dreams" and re-examine them: Were they still what I wanted now? Was I chasing something that no longer held value for me or was it what I wanted out of my one and only life?

It was a *great* year, and one that set my mind up for the next period of my life—building my own company. It also taught me something about balance.

Many times, I'm asked how I balance my life: holidays versus work, hobby versus career, competitive sport versus leisure time with my family, time socializing with friends versus time spent with colleagues, learning new skills outside of work versus those courses necessary to get new insights in your job—each a passion that could take up an eight-hour workday every day on its own. My stock answer is that there is no balance. Success is not about balancing these many components of your life—about giving each equal time—as much as it is making sure you are doing something you love. Then balance becomes not something you plan (so many hours on this and so much on that) but a blend of all the things that you care about. Of course, that still means that some weeks, months, years may be totally focused on career, whereas other years, like my trip-around-the-world year, become mostly about insight and preparation for the next phase. Balance is not something, in other words, that means resetting every day and hoping to make a forty-hour week fit into every normal twenty-four-hour day. Balance is about taking your life and assessing it to ensure that the components you need for *you* are all in there. Sometimes concurrently, sometimes sequentially...it doesn't really matter as long as you are getting what you personally need and want from the way you are living your life.

I've taken quite a few turns and experienced many twists in my life—voluntarily or not—from my early days to where I am now. Time is not just a great healer—it is also a great creator. You find out who you are through every experience, and if you are willing, you can reinvent yourself along the way. That reinvention is never a complete change. It is a slow creation of the person that you want to be, and it is a wonderful experience.

It goes without saying that, whether you are a man or a woman, every choice you make has consequences. For me, the price I paid for a very successful career and the path to eventually becoming a published author and global entrepreneur was my relationships. It took me forty-two years to find a guy who was willing to learn to play a game somewhere in between the soccer field and the tennis court. I learned that guys love having a successful woman on their arm but often proceed to tell her to stop doing the exact things that made her so successful. I cannot count the times I have heard, "Do you really have to get up so early to go to work?" or "Are you still working this late in the evening?" or "When are we going to have dinner?" (The answers to those questions were very simply put: "Yes," "Yes," and "Make it yourself"—which obviously didn't always go down so well.) I never gave up on this part of my life either, though; I just figured that eventually I would meet someone who was as prepared to listen to me as I was to him . . . and I did (just in case you were starting to feel sorry for me!). It's been worth it. Having learned from all those disappointments, I also became better able to voice what I wished for in a relationship and then applied that to voicing what I needed outside of a relationship, as well.

These days, I could probably buy a few racing camels myself—I have built a career from the early days as a secretary to being the COO of my own global company. It has taken a while—nothing happens overnight—but I feel that being a woman has never held me back. I would strongly argue that women have a tremendous amount to offer as long as we don't feel that we have to play the exact same game as the guys. Be emphatic; don't lose that "female-ness" in the process of building your career, and dare to be different and be proud of your accomplishments. It is true that many women under-value themselves compared to their male counterparts, and I am sure you hear that from other women leaders, too. I have seen it so many times: a man dares to ask for a promotion before he is really ready for the role because he truly believes that he can do the job, while a woman almost always feels that she has to have *all* the necessary skills in her bag before applying for that very same position. But as female managers, we should see those differences and guide other women on their path.

There are so many amazing young women out there—I meet more every single day. And I want to make sure that we promote them and support them, even if they don't quite feel ready; we can all use a mentor from time to time who forces us to the next stage. I am confident that women make excellent leaders and excellent managers—and would urge any one of you reading this to go out and create your own dreams. You'll have my support and my blessing.

Maria Gamb is the founder and CEO of NMS Communications, a coaching and training company. As a former Fortune 500 executive, she spent more than twenty years in the trenches of corporate America, directing and managing successful businesses valued in excess of $100 million.

Her work as a designer, product manager, and director provided her with experience working in Asia, Australia, Europe, and South America, which led her to write the Amazon bestselling book *Healing the Corporate World: How Value-Based Leadership Gets Results from the Inside Out.*

Maria's specialties include value-based leadership, gender intelligence and communication, team collaboration, and championing women in emerging leadership roles. Her belief is that we all are responsible for shifting the environment within business to a more constructive and collaborative model.

She is a sought-after professional international speaker, author, trainer, and advocate for women. She leads the charge for positively changing industry norms within organizations, groups, and governments' cabinets.

Maria's dedication to advancing women's leadership worldwide includes sitting on the Board of Advisors of Collective Changes and the California Women's Conference. She is a member of the Women's MBA International (WMBAI) association and the United Nations Association of New York (UNA-NY). Her work includes advancing women's economic development through the United Nations Development Programme (UNDP).

I didn't actually realize that my field, leadership consulting and training, is a mainly male-dominated world until I wrote my book, *Healing the Corporate World,* in 2010. As I was doing my research for the book, I discovered that most of the voices out there in the market are indeed men, mostly with a point of view that's not only masculine but nearly outright militant and formulaic. Many of the female voices in the arena were much smaller and quieter.

As a woman, I offer the field a different voice: one that is softer but not weaker. In addition, I offer additional real-life experience affecting the bottom line of multimillion-dollar corporations. Softer does *not* mean weaker nor does it always mean more feminine. Softer can simply mean more compassionate and tolerant. Gentler but still formidable.

Although it's tempting to say that businesses would be more effective if those positions were reversed, touting women as superior would just be a pendulum swing from the assumption that men are superior. I believe there is a place for both; we just need better skills and tools to create this balance of power in leadership positions and companies. It's in the best interest of corporations to reshape their environments and cultures to make them more desirable, fair places to work where the best talent is retained and flourishes. The cost of lost talent is astronomical.

What we fail to realize is that men and women have very different communication and therefore leadership styles. This can cause conflict and misunderstandings that contribute to an unhealthy and counterproductive work environment. Many men are often straight to business: They are very bottom-line focused. Strong handshakes. Nods of knowing and a whole lot of posturing. Get to the point and let's move on. On the other hand, women are often more communicative and seek to establish a relationship upon which to build a business relationship. What may seem like needless chatter is actually their basis for connecting to one another. Both styles are effective, but being able to blend both creates a much more effective environment. It's about balance, not who is better. It's neurological, not personal.

"Male" and "female" skills are naturally part of all of our makeups —each of us has greater strength in some, all, or both kinds of skills. There are plenty of super-masculine skilled women out there, as well as men with excellent softer skills. For instance, I have a masculine side to my own personality that wants to get to the issues, outline steps, and take on a course of action. In that regard, I speak the language of my male counterparts. The challenge is to create the right balance between connection (feminine skill) with those with whom you work or engage and the systematic, logistical process (masculine skills) of getting to the goal.

A balanced approach is appealing because it satisfies the internal wiring and conditioning of both genders. Yet I do have men remark that they wish to dispense with the niceties and just get to the point. Sometimes I've had women rankle at the thought of sharing anything personal. Once a woman said to me, "My dear, I don't care where you buy your shoes." (The funny thing is, unless someone else brings a detail like that up, I don't. It was her defense mechanism.) In both situations, I smiled, adjusted my cadence, and continued forward. Because, after all, what can you do but adjust on the spot? While you shouldn't ever compromise yourself, you do sometimes need to adjust your approach. It's the skill of agility and learning not to take things personally.

Feminine skills go beyond just the desire to connect. Women are the grand observers; we notice more body language, more physical cues and patterns in behavior than men do. We are also amazing record keepers; we can weave seemingly unrelated events and details into a coherent narrative that links them all together. Women are also better multitaskers. Women think about the effects of change beyond the core group with which they might be dealing. They are what I call "outward-ripple focused." These skills are very important when consulting with and training a group of individuals. It's instinct, intuition, and a processing function akin to the way many women naturally interact with others. For the most part, these are effortless skills for them.

Often, I find women believe that if they are not experienced in stereotypical hard-core masculine leadership styles that corporate life is not for them (this may be the reason that when women become entrepreneurs, they tend to set up their businesses "on the side" rather than as their chief focus). In fact, the skills women bring to the table are skills that must be integrated into any leadership role *regardless of gender*. We just happen to own these particular skills and might not realize the value of them.

The truth is that we judge one another based first on first glance of one another's exteriors. Fair or not, it's human nature. I like to take advantage of the fact that people underestimate me. I am often initially dismissed because I'm a woman and only five foot three (even though inside I'm actually a six-foot-four linebacker who just keeps going and going until I get to the goal post). "How can she know anything about any of this?" I can read it on their faces. People are polite. I am polite back. However, once they understand the breadth of my experience in business, nationally and internationally, they are more willing to listen. I think that's the benefit of being who I am in stature and gender. I could spend a lot of time taking it personally—focusing on the negative aspect of this. But I don't. It's a waste of time.

When I was younger I tried really hard to convey, and was quite effective at portraying, a very hard exterior. Trying to be someone I was not was just plain uncomfortable and unfulfilling. There comes a point where we all make the decision just to be ourselves. Embrace what others perceive, no matter what it is. Every perceived negative has a positive if you choose to see it. When you know this, then you can utilize it with integrity and make it work for you rather than against you.

My success has had everything to do with the fact that I truly believe that I'm here to help women become the leaders of their own lives. I am here to help the workplace become functional again so that there are jobs and opportunities for more people, and so parents can go home, be present with their families, and raise happy, healthy children. I never forget that that's what this is all for. It's my mission and purpose. Or on a far more condensed scale, in a few words, I'm here to help people heal their relationships with one another. Because at the end of the day, that's what this is all about: tolerance, acceptance, and peace.

As women, we need to embrace the belief that there is more than enough success to go around, rather than focusing on competing with one another. A scarcity mentality has been drummed into us from birth: "Hurry, run, compete, get there before anyone else." But I believe success has a domino effect. Once the first domino is tipped, the momentum must continue to get to the end. And so helping someone else means helping that person find and perpetuate her momentum. Remember, just because a chain of domino pieces are set up, it doesn't necessarily mean that all the pieces will automatically cause a chain reaction. Inevitably, adjustments are made. New perspectives are often deployed to figure out how to make the momentum cause each piece to fall in place. Success is the same. When we contribute our perspectives, insights, and resources to another person, we are helping them get their domino pieces in line to create a smoother, less interrupted momentum toward the realization of that dream. We are responsible *to* others but not *for* them. Ultimately, their success is in their own hands. We're just responsible for helping to get the domino pieces in place.

If I had one piece of advice to offer, it would be this:

They will tell you that you're crazy. Be it anyway.

They will judge the words you speak. Say them anyway.

They will try to rein in your wild ways. Do those things anyway.

In the process, love them regardless. Harbor no resentment. Remember, you must forgive them because they simply do not understand. You need not explain it or convince them. Let your actions show that things can be different.

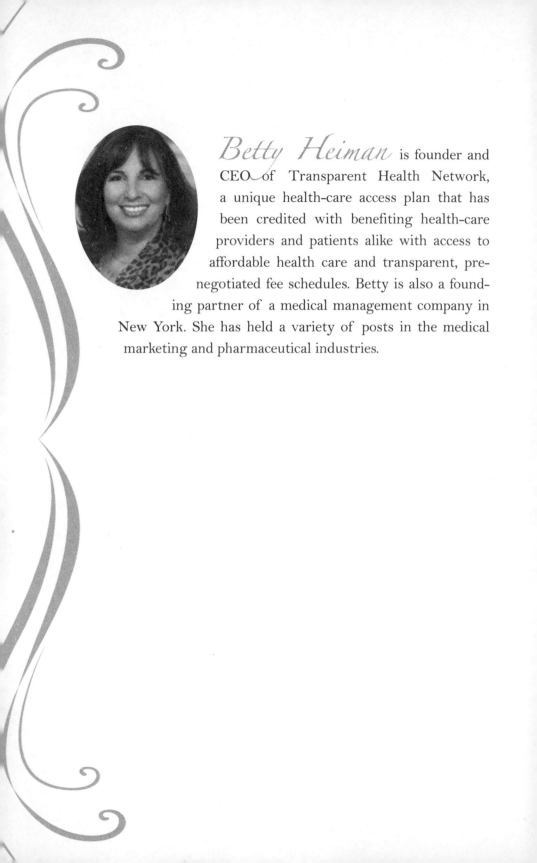

Betty Heiman is founder and CEO of Transparent Health Network, a unique health-care access plan that has been credited with benefiting health-care providers and patients alike with access to affordable health care and transparent, pre-negotiated fee schedules. Betty is also a founding partner of a medical management company in New York. She has held a variety of posts in the medical marketing and pharmaceutical industries.

I recently had an interesting discussion at a cocktail party for women in leadership roles. We started talking about whether women are being asked to join the table. By the time the evening concluded, we were in agreement that joining the table was not enough. Women need to change the shape of that table. As women, we approach problems in unique ways and with a creative spirit that allows us to see opportunities from a different point of view. However, there are times when it takes real courage to raise your hand and say, "Status quo does not work here. We need to approach this problem in a new way." Leaders succeed when they encourage creative thinking in others and have the courage to employ new strategies in the marketplace.

Where there is chaos, there is opportunity. Take a look at the health-care industry. It is well established that women are typically the purchasers of health care for their households. Yet these voices are largely absent from the boardrooms of the health-care industry and in the C-suites of insurance companies. As a result, the viewpoint of the health-care consumer is largely ignored. It is vitally important that consumers of health care (primarily women) have a clear understanding of the true cost of health-care and pharmaceutical services. Consumers must have the ability both to access and afford health care. The chaos in health care has allowed my company the ability to create a new platform for access to health care for the uninsured. In creating this platform, we recognized the needs of the true consumers of health care. And we learned that we need to find the entrepreneurial spirit to encourage women to raise their hands.

Diana Hendel is CEO of Long Beach Memorial, Community Hospital Long Beach, and Miller Children's Hospital Long Beach in California. She holds a BS in biology from the University of California–Irvine, a doctor of Pharmacy from the University of California–San Francisco, and has been an assistant clinical professor of pharmacy practice at UCSF and at the University of Southern California. She serves on the boards of several medical and civic organizations and is a frequent public speaker. Diana was among the first women selected to join the Southern California Leadership Council, a business and public policy partnership that includes four former California governors and three dozen CEOs of top Southern California companies.

Health care has traditionally attracted many women to a variety of professions. However, in the course of my career, the senior administrative roles have almost always been held by men, except for positions like chief nursing officer. That has begun to change over the past twenty years, but it is still the norm in business meetings I attend—especially meetings that aren't health care–focused—for me to be the only woman at the table or one of a very few. And it is when I am alone at the table that I see differences emerge.

I'm not certain if it is something specific about being a woman or just that I constitute a minority that changes the meeting's dynamics. I think that excluding minorities and wanting to get everyone thinking alike are just natural aspects of group dynamics, but that tendency toward homogeneity can limit what a group is capable of. If there is roughly equal distribution of sexes at a particular meeting, the behavior tends to be more experimental and derives from one's own personal experiences, but if there is a small minority of women present, or just one, then it's about being a minority within the group, in ways that might have nothing to do with any specific female or male traits.

Being the only woman in the room at a meeting of leaders and executives can be intimidating and can alter the way you think and feel about yourself.

Then there is the reality that some people still think women are not as capable or strong or as willing to take on difficult tasks as men. Yet it is important to distinguish whether we're truly being dismissed or are just projecting our fear of that. Our whole lives have been modeled around what our culture tells us it means to be a woman. It can be hard to separate the reality of what's happening from the internalized beliefs we carry into the room. (There is a powerful documentary called *Miss Representation* that I think everyone needs to see. It says a great deal about how we are taught and conditioned to see ourselves.)

Although these situations can be intimidating, I believe they've helped me become more successful. When I reflect on how I feel and react in that setting, I think I have a tendency to listen harder and also feel a responsibility to speak up more. Also, there are times when being the only woman at the table results not in my being passed over but in someone making a point of asking, "So what do you think?" But even if that doesn't happen, I long ago got into the habit of offering my opinion when it's appropriate.

Whether that's always a "woman's" opinion, I'm not so sure. Some studies out there say men and women tend to think differently. I think there are such tendencies. But my experience is that when people are working together in a room, it's more about their own personalities and opinions and less about gender. Occasionally, things come up that are more female–male oriented, but I think those are the exceptions.

Even so, it's important for women to be well represented on boards and in upper management. I think women bring different perspectives, and that can be a tremendous contribution. Women bring the other half of the whole culture, if you will. It isn't a question of whether women's perspectives are better or worse. It's that we live in a world where there are equal numbers of men and women, so to have all aspects of humanity fully expressed by both genders is healthy for a culture. So it's about everyone contributing his or her unique skills.

As for my own success, I can attribute that to several factors. As I grew up, I always felt that I could express myself and do anything I wanted to do, which gave me a nice head start. As I said earlier, many women grow up boxed in by what they are told are the ways women should think and feel and behave. They have to break out of that, but I didn't have much of a struggle in that regard.

I think there are ways of looking at myself and at the world that have been important to my success. These include being open about the attributes of men and women and not boxing myself into any category, knowing who I am and being honest about what I feel, knowing what I want out of life, knowing that what life holds for me is an ongoing process of discovery, knowing my own gifts and skill sets, and taking care of myself physically and emotionally.

I think we need to be able to find balance. When I am rested and clear minded, I am a much better leader than when I am just racing to get things done. Balance also means accepting that not everything has to be the way you think it is supposed to be. It means letting go of control, realizing that control is an illusion. This has certainly helped me to be more successful and, ultimately, to see the best in everyone around me. It is a great habit to look for what's wonderful and amazing and highly valuable in everybody else, and to enjoy the gifts that others offer.

Of course, with success comes the responsibility to help others achieve their potential as well. That starts with being willing to mentor women of any age or at any stage of their careers. I think it's important to be involved with education, with students. We need to engage with peers and staff members who are seeking mentoring—and to recognize those who aren't actively seeking mentoring but could benefit from us reaching out to them.

It is amazing how helpful it is to a person just starting out for someone older and more experienced to take an interest, listen, and offer guidance. Affirming and validating a person's career pathway can reduce fear and boost confidence. This is something I have a responsibility to do as a leader. In fact, one of the largest responsibilities I have is to make things better for the next generation. I do that by helping that next generation ascend into leadership roles.

The general advice I'd give younger women has a lot to do with knowing who you truly are and what you want out of life. Take the time to write out a mission statement, understanding that this statement can evolve and change. You don't have to share it or even read it aloud, but do come back to it from time to time to evaluate whether this is what you want to be doing at this moment in your life. Take stock of where you are. Recognize the things that you really, truly enjoy. Find what your passions are and be honest about what you don't enjoy.

Do this and you'll be less likely to get caught on the "hamster wheel" of what other people think you should be doing. It isn't about hitting milestones. It's about doing what really fulfills you.

Nadine Lajoie is a bestselling author, international speaker, championship motorcycle racer, accomplished business leader, musician, and vocalist. Born in the province of Quebec, Canada, Nadine harbored thoughts of suicide as a young woman, but she reached out for help and changed her life "one corner at a time." She now uses her success in life, business, and motorcycle racing to inspire teen and adult audiences to race toward their own dreams with passion and balance.

Nadine earned her BS in actuarial sciences in 1992 and soon launched a highly successful financial planning enterprise, semi-retiring at age 36. In 2001, she bought a motorcycle for pleasure and two years later began a successful racing career.

Nadine founded a real-estate investment firm, authored the book *Win the Race of Life with Balance and Passion at 180 MPH,* and coauthored with Les Brown the book *Fight for Your Dreams!*

Being a woman in a "man's world" is not always easy, and that's where I've been in all my lines of work—financial planner, motorcycle racer, real-estate professional, and speaker. In my experience, you have to work harder and prove yourself a little bit more than the guys. But once you are accepted by the men, as soon as you've made your mark, there are many advantages. Once we are part of the gang, people listen to us because they know that there are not that many women in their industry.

In my first three years in the financial planning business, I wasn't a good closer, but once I got better at closing, the commissions were substantial, as much as $125,000 from one client. So once you "crack the code" in building close relationships with your clients, you begin to grow exponentially. I've been a slow starter in general. Maybe you are, too. But as soon as we get into the groove or into the moment, we are recognized as powerful women, and I think people can relate to and have confidence in us.

We also have the advantage of being more intuitive and better listeners than our male counterparts. Our intuitive nature leads us to spend more time and effort on conversation and building relationships, whereas men are eager to get straight to the point. To be honest, I think I am a good mix of both of those tendencies. I can be straight to the point, but I think it is also important to connect with my clients.

I think we women tend to volunteer more of ourselves, to spend more time and effort giving advice. We spend more time with each client, in meetings and on the phone. That is not always a positive trait; sometimes it's the reason why we are underpaid. What I mean is, although it is in our nature to give, sometimes we forget about ourselves. We have a tendency to spend so much time helping others that it gets out of balance with our goals for financial freedom.

Championship motorcycle racing is really a man's world. But in 2007 I finished third in Daytona, competing against seventy-five guys. I finished ninth in the national Daytona championship, as well—I was one of five women racing in a series with 500 men. I'm sure people were thinking that it was cute to have a woman in the race. Then I'd start to pass the men, using advice they'd given me. The other racers might have thought it was luck, but it was really due to a process of focus, determination, and discipline. I applied that in sport and also in business. The biggest challenge we have as women is to get that start and get accepted for who we are. We know we've made it when they stop saying how cool it is to have a woman in the business. That's true even in the motivational speaking business. I'm still amazed that there are so few women on the big stage today. I was also surprised to read recently that only 14.5 percent of executives in Fortune 500 companies are women.

Why are we less visible? Women have the same skills and abilities as men, but we have to work harder to make our mark.

I just said we have the same skills and abilities, but there are differences between men and women in the way we behave. Sometimes I may be too vulnerable, but I think vulnerability, compassion, and understanding are good qualities to have. There were times when this vulnerability seemed out of place to others. For example, you might find me at the race track in my motorcycle jacket crying like a baby. I *am* a baby by nature, and at the same time I am a strong woman. I'm able to marry both sides together. I think that successful women are able to bring together the masculine and the feminine, to combine their spiritual, personal, and family lives with the go-getter side of themselves. When we are able to merge these aspects of our lives we can make an impact. And I think that all starts with just being your authentic self first and foremost.

So get out of your comfort zone and keep pushing harder and eventually the guys will respect you. Some men say that softness is a good quality in a woman. We need to honor that softness if it's part of who we are, but we also need to stand firm and work hard to make sure we are treated as equals.

Thinking outside the box has always come naturally to me, perhaps because that is where I have lived all my life. There has never been a box that I really fit into. When I was five years old, I knew I wanted to be a star. I always saw myself on a big stage and traveling around the world. But until the age of twenty-five, I wasn't happy or content with myself. There was a big void inside of me. I was good at sports and music. I was a good student, and I had good parents. But I still wanted to commit suicide. Why? Because I didn't fit in anywhere. I was a nerd, so the sports people didn't like me. I was a sportswoman, so other people didn't like me. I was also a musician. So that totaled three "gangs" that I was in, but I never felt that I really belonged to any of them. I had a lot of passion for volleyball and piano, and that was what kept me going. I was able to wake up every morning looking forward to playing volleyball and playing the piano.

Being an "outside the box" person—a woman who races motorcycles, for instance—has given me some special insights that I pass on to other women. Build your confidence so that you can overcome your fear and get out of your comfort zone. Be yourself, be bold, and be fast. Learn that you can be vulnerable and a go-getter at the same time. Adrenaline and spirituality go together. React fast. Be quick on your feet and adaptable in everything you do because women have to do it a bit faster than the guys. Women are naturally less inclined to "live on the edge" than men, but if we stay in our comfort zones, other people pass us and beat us to the finish line, whatever that might be—the new client, the new job, the new sale. It's about being on top of your game all the time.

To reach your full potential, reach out to get as much as you can. And think outside the box. Women tend to conform to that stereotype of caring more about family and home. However, we should all strike a balance between that and reaching for our dreams.

So rev up your engine and race against the boys. Get out on the racetrack and out of your comfort zone. Do whatever it takes and never give up, no matter how discouraged you are. Never stop competing and never stop caring about yourself.

Wendy Lea is the executive chairman of Get Satisfaction (previously, she served as the CEO of Get Satisfaction), a San Francisco–based community platform that helps companies create engaging customer experiences by fostering online conversations about their products and services at every stage of the lifecycle.

In addition to her role at Get Satisfaction, Wendy currently serves as an angel investor, strategic advisor, and board member for a long list of start-up companies. Wendy serves on the boards of Silicon Valley Social Venture Capital (SV2.org) and Corporate Visions. She has been recognized as a Top 100 Woman of Influence in Silicon Valley and received a Watermark "Women Who Made Their Mark" Award.

Prior to Get Satisfaction, Wendy was cofounder of On Target, a sales consulting firm acquired by Siebel Systems in 1999. After the acquisition, Wendy served as vice president of ebusiness consulting at Siebel Systems.

Wendy holds a BS in business administration and marketing from the University of Mississippi.

Working as the CEO of a high-growth, venture-backed start-up is exciting and stressful. There's a great deal of responsibility and accountability and pressure to meet or exceed expectations. It's a whole lot of work.

What does it feel like to be a woman doing this? Magnificent! It's enabled me to bring all of my female characteristics to my role because this business is all about the relationships between companies and their customers. Our product is software, but at the end the day, good business is all about good relationships. My feminine attributes have allowed me to bring unique energy, aspiration, and execution to that product. I also enjoy that it is a social-media product that allows me to be very expressive.

Just as there are advantages to being a woman in this business, there are also challenges. I am very emotional and I tend to take things personally. I don't like to disappoint people. Those may be specific Wendy Lea characteristics, but I see them as related to my feminine side. Fortunately, over the years I've developed a very complementary skill that helps balance some of my more feminine qualities—I am extremely courageous. I draw on my courage to get amped up to overcome my emotional reactions. It's mind over matter. My head can override my feelings, and when it does, I am better at my job. The best scenario is when I can *integrate* my head and heart because then my beliefs come across in a more profound and compelling way—those are the moments when I shine as a leader.

There are other challenges many women face in this business. For example, I don't always pattern match very well with men. It's not that they don't respect or support me; it's just that I don't fit the stereotypical box in the venture capital world. Venture investors are constantly trying to see if you are the "bull's-eye" person they can invest in. I don't have an engineering degree; I'm not under thirty, I didn't go to MIT. I am a sixty-year-old woman with a marketing degree. They know I'm successful, but I just don't look like everyone else they do business with and that sometimes causes tension and concern. It's not a factor that can't be overcome, but it does present an extra challenge that probably wouldn't be an issue if I fit into the standard "box" venture capitalists are accustomed to dealing with. The differences aren't just aesthetic; I behave differently than my male colleagues by being more open and transparent and allowing myself to be vulnerable. I don't see that in many men.

I am a driven person, but money and recognition are not what drive me. I am driven to complete the task, to reach the goal, and to do so in a way that achieving that goal can be shared with others to get them excited.

Success is a tough formula to crack. Mine can be mostly attributed to drive, vision, and an ability to act as a great synthesizer. It's natural for me to look at market details and competitive details and bring them together quickly to support a vision. I don't think of myself much as an innovator; my talent is being able to match up trends and translate them into a vision to push things forward. Part of that talent draws on my skills as a forward observer, much like a scout sent out to find out what's happening ahead. One of my greatest strengths is excellent communication combined with my unrelenting commitment to authenticity. Each of those qualities are woven into the tapestry of my leadership style—strong and interconnected.

Everybody talks about the ability to collaborate as a skill set that comes naturally to women. It's true, but "collaboration" tends to be overused and sometimes get hijacked by people (women included) who don't really understand the concept. To me, collaboration is an explicit recognition and leverage of the needs of others. If you cannot see the interdependency of needs in a team, it is impossible to collaborate. Then you need people to trust you, and that trust has to be explicit. When you have all that, you are able to engage in joint decision making and creative problem solving that others will execute. If I could find more people who had that skill—who could collaborate and execute in a way that exceeded expectations—I would hire them in an instant. Unfortunately, sometimes our emotions get in the way and we don't get the clarity we need to be an effective collaborator. In addition, it's important to work on developing a wider range of collaboration styles. I think women have broader range than men, but we need to apply it more. If I could find more people who could do that, they would all be in my business.

I am fortunate to be surrounded by female entrepreneurs. I know there are not enough women in the boardroom, but I can look in any direction and easily find a woman who is building a business. I don't feel isolated because I actively seek out women to help me with different aspects of my business. I'm surrounded by a like-minded tribe here in Silicon Valley and do my best to take advantage of this unique ecosystem by building my network whenever and wherever I can.

Everybody talks about paying it forward; I have a formula for it. For the last decade, I have devoted 10 percent of my time every week to helping other women accomplish their objectives. Those women have been young and old, ranging from bootstrapped and venture-backed entrepreneurs to big corporations and brands. The important part is that I pass on what has and hasn't worked for me, something I feel responsible and accountable for. I hope I am able to inspire and inform others in the process.

Sharon Lechter is the CEO and founder of Pay Your Family First, a licensed CPA, CGMA, author, businesswoman, investor, international speaker, financial literary activist, and philanthropist. She is the author of *Think and Grow Rich for Women* and *Save Wisely, Spend Happily*, and coauthor of the international bestseller *Rich Dad Poor Dad* and fourteen other Rich Dad books, *Three Feet from Gold*, and *Outwitting the Devil*. Her company, Pay Your Family First, is dedicated to providing financial educational resources to families everywhere. She created the award-winning life and money reality game *ThriveTime for Teens*, used to educate young people around the world.

Sharon was appointed to the President's Advisory Council on Financial Literacy in 2008. The council served both President George Bush and President Barack Obama, advising them on the need for financial literacy.

In 2008, Sharon was appointed to the National CPA Financial Literacy Commission as a national spokesperson for financial literacy. She is a member of the business advisory board for EmpowHER, a company dedicated to women's health issues. Sharon also serves on the national board of the Women Presidents' Organization and the national board of Childhelp, a national organization founded to prevent and treat child abuse.

For more than twenty years, I have been an entrepreneur dedicated to financial literacy. I have been able to combine my passion for promoting the need for financial education with my skills as an accountant and my talent in the publishing industry.

I believe that we are all the CEOs of our lives, no matter what our gender. There have been times in my career when I have made decisions that were best for the business or the mission at hand, even though they were not the best for my personal career. That's what CEOs do and I submit that in order to move forward with your career in particular and your life in general, you must weigh the options as they are presented and sometimes make tough calls.

For example, my success has been a culmination of my professional and personal experiences. Accounting was my career choice because I wanted to succeed in business and I recognized that understanding financial statements and the stories they told would be an important skill to learn. I also recognized that whether I stayed in the accounting field or became an entrepreneur, both would allow me to have more flexibility in controlling my own schedule when and if I chose to have children.

I started in my career in public accounting in 1976 at a time when there were very few women in the field. I began work for a Big Eight accounting firm (back in the day when there was a Big Eight) in Atlanta, Georgia. Most of my audit assignments were companies in small towns in Georgia—all owned and led by men. I remember one owner of a calcite mine greeting me by saying, "I am not sure why you are here, Missy. I don't need a secretary and I don't need my windows washed."

Do you think he would have said the same thing to a male accountant?

At that moment, I had a choice. I could get angry and alienate the client, I could cry, or I could respond without engaging. Yet I chose to respond with, "This is good news, Harry, because I am a lousy secretary, and I don't do windows. But if you want your bank loan next month, you and I are going to become good friends."

How did he respond? He laughed and we worked together for several years. He had three daughters and his bark was, indeed, worse than his bite. The term "sexual discrimination" wasn't even used at that time. I and my fellow female accountants just recognized that we needed to work hard—often harder—than our male counterparts.

Thankfully, times have changed. Today, more than half of graduating accountants are women. We've come a long way!

In a past era, women professionals were also often challenged by an environment in which successful women were not generally very helpful to other women coming up through the ranks. In fact, they were often hostile to them. I am happy to say that I have seen this change dramatically in the last ten years, with more and more professional women serving as mentors to younger women, as well as the creation of many women's groups that serve as peer-to-peer support.

I think women in general are better collaborators than men. My experience in my field has been that men are more driven by elevating their egos and self-advancement while women concentrate on client satisfaction. And although I know many men who are equally passionate about financial education, I believe women are better equipped with the patience necessary to create change in both the education system and the political arena.

As a natural collaborator, I have built great teams that have taken a vision and turned it into a successful business. Bringing people with different talents together and leading them through the development of innovative solutions to various business needs creates an environment and a culture of success. This has been particularly helpful in my advocacy for financial education.

It is difficult, at best, to effect change in the educational system. Yet I was determined to make a difference. During the early days of my efforts, my dear friend Deborah stepped up to support my efforts financially because of her deep faith in my ability to create needed change in financial education. Her confidence and faith in me both as a friend and financially deeply affected me and drove my passion to even greater heights.

Through collaboration, I was able to bring representatives from the private sector, the banking sector, educators, and state politicians together to successfully pass legislation in the State of Arizona to highlight the importance of financial education for high school graduates.

I'd like to suggest that successful experienced women and those just entering a field collaborate to ensure we all are the best that we can be.

For those experienced women:

- Become a mentor to younger women.
- Lead by example.
- Create a path lined with encouragement and opportunities for advancement for younger women.
- Allow younger women to learn from your mistakes so they can accelerate their own success.

For those young women entering the workforce:

- Focus on your goals, continue to be a lifelong learner.
- Seize every opportunity to add value to others.
- Make different choices tomorrow if you are unhappy where you are today.

For *all* women:

- Recognize the elements that make up personal success.

I share my Personal Success Equation in my book *Think and Grow Rich: Three Feet from Gold:* $[(P + T) \times A \times A] + F =$ Your Personal Success Equation. It stands for combining your **P**assion and your **T**alent with the right **A**ssociations and the right **A**ctions plus having **F**aith in yourself and in your business. If you can do that, you're sure to generate success for your business and your life.

Marina Lee is a serial entrepreneur and tech start-up community builder. She is the founder of Women In Tech Network and Startups Edge—organizations that create dynamic platforms and promote technology growth. Through WIT Network, her mission is to provide forums to cultivate the tech start-up ecosystem between investors and entrepreneurs that will achieve more gender balance as well as attracting new funds for women ecosystems.

Marina's background includes creating and producing a highly successful radio show that focuses on world-renowned thought leaders such as Sir Richard Branson, Dr. Deepak Chopra, Robert Kiyosaki (bestselling coauthor of the Rich Dad, Poor Dad series), and Ken Blanchard (bestselling author of *One Minute Manager*).

Marina experienced success with her first business endeavor at age twenty-five. For the past ten years, she has worked on the service side of technology, assisting small to midsize companies with SAS. In addition, she is serving on the board of directors for C & Company and is a contributor to *Entrepreneur* magazine, *Business Daily News*, and *The Glass Hammer*.

Los Angeles has experienced
an explosive growth in the tech industry in 2012 and 2013. According to Intuit's Startup Ecosystem Report, LA's digital start-ups aren't just keeping pace with past performances, they are exceeding them: a total of over $1 billion was raised for the first time in 2013, a bump up from 2012, when $871 million was raised. Additionally, the twenty-five digital start-ups acquired in 2013 by other companies, including Verizon, Target, and Intuit, generated over $1.1 billion. The Walt Disney Company and Techstars have officially announced the Disney Accelerator to shine a spotlight on LA's tech start-up community. In addition, Turner/Warner Bros Media Camp, a comprehensive accelerator, has been seeking content start-ups in Hollywood as well as Santa Monica.

As innovative and fast-growing as the technology industry often is, women are still a minority. According to one venture capitalist, "In the last two or three years, I've seen more women-run businesses or women-men cofounded businesses than I had seen in my entire career." Investors estimate there are several dozen new tech companies created and run by women in Southern California. These include women-led start-ups that have raised $700,000 to $50+ million in the LA tech start-up ecosystem. There are women-led start-ups that have raised $5 to $25 million in their first rounds of funding and/or exited their companies for $50 to $800+ million in Silicon Valley. A few women-led US companies have more than $1 billion in valuation, including Care.com (Sheila Lirio Marcelo, founder, chairman & CEO), Gilt Groupe (Alexis Maybank and Alexandra Wilkis Wilson, cofounders), Eventbrite.com (Julia Hartz, cofounder), and LA-based OneKingsLane.com (Susan Feldman, cofounder). Two major accelerators that churn out $50 million to billion-dollar companies in Silicon Valley have also been taking steps toward supporting women. According to *Tech Crunch*, 500 Startups

Accelerator is launching its first syndicate in 2014, just for female founders, and Y Combinator Launch Fest spotlighted Y Combinator's first Female Founders Conference on March 1, 2014.

Initiatives like this are a start, but we have a long way to go. *Less than 7 percent of the tech start-ups currently being funded belong to women.* Therefore, LA tech leaders and a coalition of women in tech created a hub, the Women In Tech Network (WITNetwork.com), to give everyone who has an incredible idea a chance to get funded more than 7 percent of the time.

I don't, personally, like to view myself as a woman in the industry but rather as someone who gets the job done. In this technology innovation-driven environment, we pride ourselves on being problem solvers. Solutions need to be extremely simple so the end users will adapt to them quickly. We are in it to make a contribution and to create solutions for our world's problems. As the saying goes, "the bigger the problems, the bigger the solutions."

However, as women, I believe we do think differently—for the better. Numerous studies have documented how having female C-level executives and/or members of the board of directors increases companies' bottom lines. One study sponsored by the Chubb Corportation indicated that the correlation between gender diversity on boards and corporate performance can be found across most industries, from consumer discretionary to information technology. Women have great advantages if we are productive and connected.

I've seen interesting patterns in how women and men deal with their work, both during the day and after. The majority of men are more willing and ready to delegate. By contrast, I had a fear of delegating. I was always worried that if I delegated tasks or projects, the work wouldn't be done properly. Instead, I micromanaged my team and that did not get me far. I have learned to build a loyal team so I can trust them with anything—that was my solution to my personal challenge.

Most men can leave their work after a full's day work, but women tend to carry their work worries with them. I used to be a workaholic. Note that I used the past tense. I routinely worked more than twelve hours per day and it eventually affected my health. Due to a near-death experience two years ago, I have learned to balance my life. I am able to keep my work hours and time with my family separate for the most part. That's a work in progress.

Working in technology sometimes feels like a thrill ride, and this is truly an exciting time in the technology field, as we see many women in leadership roles. With sufficient funding, competence, and some good luck, the sky is the limit for women who are interested in the technical, business, and marketing side of all tech and tech start-up-related fields.

I have two big tips and recommendations for success:

First, **get support from other influential women *and* men.** Yes, there are some women who won't help. Some of them may just pay lip service toward "paying it forward" to other women. However, you can find those who are genuine if you are looking.

At WITNetwork.com, we have been fortunate to find incredible and amazing women who have helped us create and build the infrastructure and run all the moving parts of our organization. And we have been able to call upon our friends, influential women and men, to help us spread the word and provide us the contacts we need to prosper. In addition, we are also grateful for our key contributors and advisors, women and men who have been generous and gracious with their time. We appreciate each and every person who has been helping to build WIT Network to be a resounding success and beyond.

Second, **have great role models.** Most self-made powerful women inspire me! I believe Marissa Mayer, CEO at Yahoo!, and Sheryl Sandberg, COO at Facebook, have been headliners over the recent years. Other women, like Carol Ann Bartz, the former president and CEO of Yahoo!, have paved the way for those of us who are traveling on the same road now.

Some other role models include:

- Wendy Lea, CEO of Get Satisfaction (a community platform that helps companies create engaging customer experiences by fostering online conversations about their products and services), is another role model of mine, and I was fortunate to hear her personal story in Santa Monica, California. I could relate to so much of who she is and what she's experienced. Wendy said that the reason she doesn't get the results she desires is usually not because she is a woman but because women are underfunded and not treated with the respect we deserve in the Los Angeles and San Francisco tech start-up ecosystem. Especially because of that, Wendy feels the need to help when she can, and I feel the same need.

- Mary Barra is the CEO at General Motors—the first female CEO of a major automotive manufacturer. Barra broke the glass ceiling and it was certainly a historic day.
- Sheila A. Penrose, the chairman of the board for Jones Lang LaSalle (and yes, she prefers the "*Chairman*" title).
- Three very high-profile women and leaders on the world stage: Christine Lagarde at the IMF, German Chancellor Angela Merkel, and Margaret Chan, director-general of the World Health Organization. They certainly aren't alone on that world stage: President Obama's choices of Janet Yellen as chairman of the Federal Reserve and Penny Pritzker as Commerce Secretary has put women in two prestigious and very visible positions. I also admire Dilma Vana Rousseff, the President of Brazil, and Helle Thorning-Schmidt, the Prime Minister of Denmark.

At WITNetwork.com, we feature and enthusiastically advocate placing the spotlight on a myriad of amazing and incredible professional women who inspire us across all industries in national publications. We also propel and further brand women on major speaking platforms in United States and abroad.

It's about time!

We are stronger together! We are doing great things together! Together, we are here to change the world!

Jenni Luke, as chief executive officer of Step Up, directs the organization's objective of inspiring women to inspire girls. Step Up propels girls from under-resourced communities to fulfill their potential by empowering them to become confident, college bound, career focused, and ready to join the next generation of professional women. Jenni sits on the advisory board for the Conference on Girls' Education and frequently speaks on mentorship and various topics affecting women and girls. Jenni came to Step Up from within the nonprofit sector, having worked with The Alliance for Children's Rights and the ACLU of Southern California. She began her career in law and focused on social justice issues. Jenni holds a juris doctor from the University of Colorado School of Law and a bachelor's degree from the University of California–San Diego.

In my first year with Step Up, during our Inspiration Awards, I watched from backstage as some of the Step Up girls were recognized for their accomplishments. Two of the graduating seniors and their mentors shared the stage. As the girls told the audience that they were going to college and would be the first in their families to do so, they received a standing ovation from the crowd of 800 guests. When they returned backstage, they started to cry. They were overwhelmed that a room full of people, most of whom they had never met, was cheering them on. The girls recognized that they were supported by a cohesive community of women and that the community honored all that the two had been trying to accomplish.

It was a beautiful moment, experiencing the joy of these girls in celebrating their own accomplishments, but recognizing it was all the more special because of the power of community. It was a wonderful reminder of both why I'm in the nonprofit sector and how privileged I am to do the work that I do.

Most people think of a career in the nonprofit sector as the ultimate exercise in giving. But in my experience, it is more about receiving. As the leader of a nonprofit organization with more than 130,000 supporters across the country and counting, I am in a position to be the recipient of people's generosity every day. Our board members, volunteers, and countless partners give their time, talent, and treasure in innumerable ways. It is my job to turn what we've received into impact.

Nonprofit work is challenging. The great news is that I have the opportunity to involve many different constituencies and stakeholders in helping to solve community-based problems. That means it is inherently collaborative and requires a lot of consensus building. In trying to increase the high school graduation and college acceptance rates of girls in under-resourced communities, we're working with the girls, their parents or caregivers, schools, our network of professional women mentors, corporate partners—the list goes on and on. I don't lead with an eye toward 100 percent agreement, but I do always try to include input from as many different people as possible. There is a sense of ownership that people have in nonprofits and being able to harness that is the source of the organizations' strength. Inclusiveness requires patience, grace, and focus. Individuals working for nonprofits also need creative thinking skills and the ability to don numerous hats because nonprofits are, thanks to budget constraints, always trying to do more with less.

Though Step Up itself is an organization that is by and for women and girls, men are an important constituency for us. We have a large category of men we informally call the "men who get it," who support our initiatives, attend our events, and share our work with the women in their networks. Engaging men in the conversation about moving women and girls forward is crucial. I hope to do more of it as we grow.

Lisabeth Marziello, for more than twenty years, has held executive leadership positions in the Boys & Girls Clubs of America (BGCA) movement. A graduate of Whittier College, the Distinguished Level Academy of the Boys & Girls Clubs of America, and advanced training at the University of Michigan's Ross School of Business, Lisabeth has applied her talents in financial management and human resources with a passion for supporting youth.

Lisabeth and her husband, Joseph Marziello, have received national recognition as a successful CEO team. Described as a "Governance Partnership that Works" by the National Center for Nonprofit Boards, Lisabeth and Joseph continuously strive to improve the lives of children who attend BGCA activities. Lisabeth has earned many accolades, among them BGCA's 2011 Regional and National Executive of the Year and the *Portland Business Journal*'s "Most Admired CEOs" for the state of Oregon. Lisabeth and Joseph have also been highlighted in the July 2011 national edition of BoardSource's magazine. Most recently, Lisabeth serves with her husband as co-CEO for Boys & Girls Clubs of Philadelphia, working to transform this 126-year-old organization.

My husband Joseph and I have worked together as CEOs for Boys & Girls Clubs across the United States for twenty-three years. In its 2012 Philanthropy 400 report, *The Chronicle of Philanthropy* ranked BGCA eighteenth among all nonprofit organizations. Additionally, BGCA was ranked number one among youth organizations for the twentieth consecutive year.

It is a unique working relationship, and one that has been great for us both. I've known of women who have worked with their spouse or significant other, and their mind-set was that the man was "the boss." In our case, we have equal shares of responsibilities. We are equal in salary and in everything that we do. I feel that he complements my strengths and vice versa. (Seeing my parents work together and respect each other served as great training for me in this respect. They were both presidents/CEOs of companies in California where I grew up. My mom was the president/CEO of a company called Ridgewood Development and my dad was the president/CEO of Rampart General, both successful construction companies. As an entrepreneur, my dad later owned two teams in the United States Football League [USFL], and my mom was very actively involved as well.)

I have not always worked in the nonprofit sector, however. I began my career in the corporate world, working in the advertising industry for three top advertising firms. Although I worked with a few other women, it was very much a predominately male-oriented environment. For example, another woman colleague and I were a media planning team to create new ideas for the company, and we were given actual clients to help build their brand. For part of our plan, I designed a concept that received great recognition from the upper echelon of the company. Unfortunately, I didn't get the full credit for the project. Instead, it was given to the male account executive who worked with the actual clients at the time. But I don't feel bad about the situation; I view it as a great learning experience

Today, I have been working in the Boys & Girls Club movement for more than twenty-three years, and I like to think of myself as a role model for other women in the nonprofit area. My chief focus, transforming organizations through fund-raising, board development, marketing brand awareness, and program development, is a hard job. It's important, in asking for financial support, that one stay true to the organization and ensure that donors know why they should invest in the Boys & Girls Clubs—and the return on their investment. People are taking a risk when they donate; it's important that they know that you are a trustworthy steward of their financial support and will report on the outcome of their donation. Those who donate to nonprofits are donating to help improve the lives of others; therefore, they are not getting anything tangible in return, but they do receive the knowledge that their investment is going to make a difference in the world. For most donors, it is about investing in people's lives.

The same is often true in business, where you invest both funds and time. When we review resumes, we look for candidates who want to do more with their lives, not the ones who are just taking the easy road. Work ethic is very important. We look for candidates who are motivated, smart, teachable, and really want to learn, even if they don't have direct experience in the position we're offering. They often become some of the best Boys & Girls Club associates in our organization. And when they leave for pivotal roles at other Boys & Girls Clubs, it's great to know that we are helping them to build a base of great knowledge and skills that prepares them for success. It's wonderful, too, to see those same women share opportunities with other women who may not have received those opportunities otherwise.

My advice for women is the following:

- Be confident and know that you're smart.
- Stand tall and walk tall.
- Be knowledgeable about your business.

- Be passionate. Take a job that you are passionate about and that people can see that passion in your work every day.
- Make your voice heard.
- Read as much as you can and be an active participant in what's going on around you.
- Don't worry about what anybody is thinking; share your ideas. Be bold!

I really believe that if you work hard and put your mind to it, you can be anything you want to be! When you walk into the room and know that you will **make a change for the better**, you can move forward, beyond the butterflies you may feel in your stomach. Be brave!

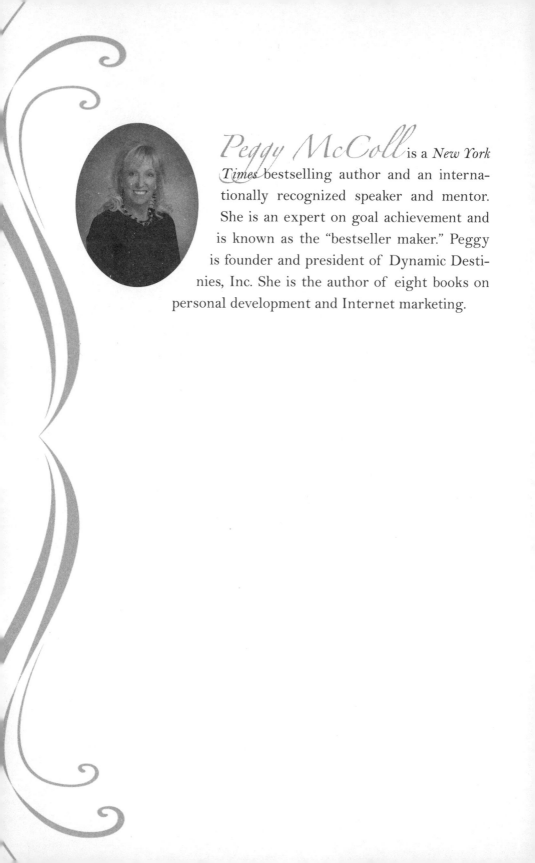

Peggy McColl is a *New York Times* bestselling author and an internationally recognized speaker and mentor. She is an expert on goal achievement and is known as the "bestseller maker." Peggy is founder and president of Dynamic Destinies, Inc. She is the author of eight books on personal development and Internet marketing.

When I was a little girl, my family used to call me "the brat" on account of my tenacity. When I had trouble getting what I wanted, I would find a way to make things happen. I was always able to do that. It was no different when I started out in my career, completely driven to achieve certain goals. In fact, the third book I wrote is called *Be a Dog with a Bone*. The concept is that we should hold onto our dreams with the tenacity of a dog with a bone and not let anyone take them away from us. But when I wrote my first book, I had no idea what I was getting into. I just assumed that if I wrote a great book, the buyers would come. So I wrote my book and self-published it and offered it to the world and *nothing happened*.

I went to a conference on book marketing to find out where I went wrong. I heard someone there say that writing your book is 5 percent of the work—95 percent of the work is the marketing. So I went after the marketing like. . .a dog with a bone. I had a big launch party and went to work.

That is a great example of walking the talk in my own career. It's what we mean by authenticity. It's a quality you see in so many successful women—like Mary Morrissey, who I got to know a couple of years ago after we met at a Transformational Leadership Council meeting in Arizona. Mary runs a very successful business called LifeSOULutions. Soon after we met, she and I started a business called Making a Million Look Small, and she is now one of my closest friends. She is an impressive woman. She cares deeply about her customers and their experiences. She delivers value beyond anything I've seen before. Mary really does walk her talk. That's authenticity.

Being authentic also means being true to who you are, and for women that means using and developing our feminine traits and skills. For example, I would say that we women express our emotions a little bit more than men. Most of us are gentler in our approach.

In my work, I probably relate to clients with more compassion and empathy than men typically would. The men I've worked with tend to be more direct and sometimes come across as less sensitive than women.

When I do relate to people with empathy and compassion, when I really connect with what they're going through, that enables me to help them achieve their desired results. People value that and cherish it. That produces a lot of referrals in my business. My clients tell others about me because they know that I genuinely care, that I am authentic and not a big phony-baloney. When I tell the stories of when I was divorced and a single mom, how I went through that challenging time building a successful business and turned my life around, people say, "If she can do it, I can do it!" That has helped a great many people and has contributed much to my success.

Making myself open and vulnerable can have its drawbacks, especially given that I market on the Internet. The 'net is a wonderful thing, but it exposes us to both positive and negative dialog. Some people are highly suspicious by nature, don't believe what they read, and post comments that are untrue or, well, *not nice* on social media. I am a very sensitive person. And sometimes the more visible and open and transparent you are, the nastier people get. I remember author Mark Victor Hansen saying, "The higher you rise, the more people will throw stones at you." As I became more successful in my career, I realized this was true. We're all human and we all have feelings. My biggest challenge has been dealing with that aspect of public exposure, but if you're going to be authentic, then you have to learn to live with that one negative consequence among all the wonderful ones.

And believe me, there is nothing more wonderful than helping someone turn her life around. I met a woman named Anick through our children. Anick was in a dysfunctional marriage, and she wanted to have her own business so that she could be independent. She had some formal education and didn't feel that she had any of what it takes to create a successful business. She didn't believe in herself and was full of fear. So she started to study with me and built up a great deal of self-confidence. She broke through that fear and opened up a couple of fitness centers that are now highly successful. Now she is remarried and living in a new house. She just lives an extraordinary life.

Anick studied passionately. She was so hungry for information that she set apart some time *each day* to learn and to apply positive messages and ideas to her life until she was ready to open that first fitness center.

That's what I love about my work. I feel that I am a difference maker. The work that I'm doing in this world has a great ripple effect. I help someone who goes on to help another—the effect is exponential. For example, my becoming a self-help author and speaker has instilled the desire in others to do similar kinds of work. They approach me and ask me to teach them to how to do it. So when I help one other person, it ultimately helps many others. In the early 90s, I established a mission statement: "Making a positive contribution to the lives of millions." I can live by that statement because of the way the message radiates outward from person to person.

There is so much we can all do to help people every day, even people we've never met. We can do it through blogs and social media. People in my profession can do it through newsletters, books, and audio and video programs. We can create coaching programs and work with people intimately. We are not in competition with each other. We collaborate together to help each other, and when I help someone else rise up, we all rise. Few women have the big stage I have today, but we can all do things like this in our daily lives. So, please give, because the more you give, the more you get back. It's the law of the universe.

The best advice I've been given is to script your life as you choose it to be. Literally script it. Write it out in the present tense and include all the details. I call this "power life scripting." In a power life script, I talk about *who I am* as well because it is not enough just to create a vision of how we want our lives to be. We have to *be* the person who is living that life. So that script needs to contain "I am" statements. Women should script it all out and then step into that vision and be that person they see themselves being. I have done that, and it has contributed the most to my success. I even recorded my script. I've got an audio track in my own voice, really excited. Now I can plug my iPhone into my car and push "play" and *wow!*

The more that we are really living, feeling, and being the person we have *chosen* to be, the more success we will attract in our lives. So that's what I would suggest: Script out your life, write it in the present tense, and make sure the words you choose are positive words only.

Ursula Mentjes founded the sales training firm Sales Coach Now in 2004. She is an inspirational speaker, best-selling author, and certified sales coach who specializes in neurolinguistic programming (NLP) to help her clients increase their sales.

Ursula grew up on a farm in Minnesota, learning the value of hard work and entrepreneurship at a very early age. In 1996, she graduated from St. Olaf College with a degree in psychology and communication. A few months later, she took a sales job with a computer training company in hope of earning enough money to go to law school. Instead, she found such success in sales that she rose to the position of president of the company by the age of twenty-seven.

Ursula is also the bestselling author of *Selling with Intention, Selling with Synchronicity,* and *One Great Goal.* She was president of the National Association of Women Business Owners–California and has held numerous other offices in that organization. She is a founding member of the networking and educational organization Business Resources Connection and 2013 recipient of the Willow Tree Extraordinary Entrepreneur Award.

Being a woman in my line of
work means everything to me. My passion is to help entrepreneurs
and sales professionals make lots of money so that they can give to
the organizations they care about and live great lives. That is my
mission and the thing that gets me up every morning.

When I started as a sales professional, there weren't many
women executives at the top. I wanted very much to become the
president of a company, and by the age of twenty-seven I was. After
that company was sold, I went out on my own to train entrepreneurs
and sales professionals on how to grow their sales. I had learned
how to "sell with intention" and had all these great tools to share that
were different from conventional wisdom. I did research on books
about sales and found that there were a lot of great books written by
men but few by women. I thought that was a niche I could fill, but
it pleases me to find that my books appeal to both women and men.
Even today, there is novelty in being a woman in my field—it always
surprises people.

My approach to sales training grows out of my feminine traits,
and yet it works for both sexes. I think men appreciate a sense of
femininity and softness. In the past, men thought that sales had to
be a win–lose game—that it had to be hard and tough. Either you
beat the customer or the customer beats you. The guys who come to
my classes are tough men, but they love the softer side of selling, being able to build relationships with their clients and still get the sale.
They tell me that the sales process becomes easier for them. That is
something that I bring as a woman—the idea that selling can be easy
and that it's about helping people: a win–win proposition.

I know that being a woman brings special challenges to many of
us, but that doesn't have to be the case. I believe that you can create whatever you want to create and put your stake in the ground
as a leader. It is a benefit to me to be a woman because there are so

many women business owners now. Women are starting businesses at twice the rate that men are.

Some women feel they have to behave a certain way, to act like men, to be successful. I think it is absolutely necessary to be *who you are*, and as a woman, that means embracing my femininity. I dress "professionally feminine." Right now, I look particularly feminine, given that I am eight months pregnant, but I can walk on stage with confidence and be received the way I always am. People say to me that I am the same person on stage that I am "behind the scenes." I take that seriously.

No matter what, you have to be yourself. I do a lot of speaking across the country, and the feedback I get is that people feel that they can connect with me. I am not intimidating. People can talk to me without shame about their businesses and what's not working in their sales efforts because I am willing to share my challenges, too. My ability to be authentic gives people permission to be themselves, too.

One of my mentors is Loral Langemeier, who has had five books on the *New York Times* bestsellers list. She is definitely not afraid to sell, and she is someone I have been able to watch closely and learn from. She had to overcome many obstacles, starting out in a male-dominated field. Now she is well accepted and has blazed a trail for women following her. When I first started putting on live events, I wanted Loral to be one of my speakers. I knew she was very picky about speaking engagements, that they had to be truly worth her time. I remember meeting her and asking her in person to speak at one of my events. I had already sent the dates to her team. It turned out she was scheduled to be Australia at the time of my event, so I asked her if she would speak on another date. She finally agreed. Later on, in writing the foreword to one of my books, she mentioned how I had had the guts to keep asking her to come and speak at my event. Looking back, I realized what a big step that was for me to take. It helped me to become more confident in what I was doing. Loral has had a profound effect on my business.

Today, I try to help men and women in business by connecting them to speaking opportunities. It's one way of paying forward what people like Loral did for me. And of course, my whole business is based on sharing wisdom that has been passed down to me.

Three things lie at the core of this. The first is *be authentic*. There are times we are afraid of that, but when we are our most authentic selves, we get more business than we ever imagined. Second, *believe in yourself*. If you don't, no one else will. This is one of the most important parts of being successful in sales, along with believing in your products and services. When people *feel* that belief, they will buy from you. Third, *take bold and inspired action*. You've got to get off the couch. Once we are clear on what we want, we have to go out and ask people for help and for opportunities. Success isn't just handed to us. Good things come to those who step out.

Lauren E. Miller, founder of Stress Solutions University, an international motivational speaker, and an award-winning and bestselling author, has been recognized nationally and internationally, including in *Success, Redbook, Ladies' Home Journal, Family Circle,* and the *International Journal of Healing and Care* and on networks such as Discovery Channel, Lifetime, CNBC, and MSNBC. Through Stress Solutions University, bimonthly live stress-relief hot-seat video calls, workshops, conferences, and one-to-one programs, Lauren equips people globally with mind-set skills and physiological techniques to de-stress their lives, regain inner clarity, and step into personal excellence. Enjoy a free stress relief gift at www.StressSolutionsUniversity .com. For more information on Lauren, please visit her websites: www.laurenemiller.com, www.stresssolutions madeeasy.com, and www.5MinutestoStressRelief.com.

Five years ago, I was diagnosed with advanced-stage breast cancer. I experienced a double mastectomy, sixteen chemotherapies with an additional year of chemo, six weeks of daily radiation, a staph infection that almost took my life, and twelve surgeries due to third-degree burns on my chest. On the day my body was finally relieved of all medication that had been used to treat my cancer, I pushed back my furniture and proceeded to do a happy dance of gratitude around the living room. It had been a long journey to this moment—not only of healing but also of learning to find and embrace my true identity as a woman.

I was at the top of my game in life when I was diagnosed with cancer and given a 50 percent chance of survival. I had a second-degree black belt from the World Tae Kwon Do Federation and had recently won the silver medal in the Colorado State Tae Kwon Do Championship. I was working as a life coach, training my clients in spiritual, mental, emotional, and physical personal excellence. However, it was also one week before my final divorce court date, and a very stressful time in my life.

Studies continue to reveal a strong connection between stress and disease; I experienced this connection firsthand, and it gave me an opportunity to change my outlook on stress. Stress is simply a signal within your body, giving you the opportunity to identify and adjust your perception of any situation in life. You can begin again at any moment. The choice is yours, to stress or not to stress, and your choice of response to events around you will make all of the difference in the outcome. I found this to be true many times during the course of my cancer treatment and had many opportunities to practice adjusting my perceptions.

After going through the first six rounds of chemotherapy, my son found me crying on my knees in my room when I saw myself bald for the first time. He snuck up behind me, put his little hands on my head, and said, "Mom, don't cry…your soul still has hair." It was true. My soul still had hair, and it remained complete, regardless of any temporary setbacks in life. Remembering this gave me profound strength and clarity around my true identity as a woman. No matter what shifted physically about my outer appearance, the essence of my femininity and identity as a beautiful woman remained untouched and complete. I didn't have hair or breasts, but I could see, hear, walk, laugh, express myself verbally, hug my children, and, most important, love God, other people, and myself (with or without hair and breasts).

I remember one time when I was bald and breastless, standing in the grocery store line surveying the magazines. I noticed how much of my experience of feeling feminine revolved around hair and breasts. Each magazine displayed hair and breasts, breasts and hair. When I took back my ability to define myself and thought, *Even though I am bald and breastless, I am willing to love and accept myself just as I am,* a certain freedom erupted within me. My hair has grown back and I have some semblance of breasts, but I am still living in the truth that I am not my breasts or my hair. Who I am remains intact, no matter what happens outside of me.

I have noticed that my concern for what other people think stifles my ability to love and accept myself just as I am. This concern fuels a daily prayer of mine: "Dear God, protect me from compliments and complaints that I may remain grounded in the mission for which my heart beats." I notice that, as I release my concern about the response of those around me, my ability to create and inspire is limitless because it is not distracted and fragmented by worry and self-interest. The radical changes to my physical appearance gave me the opportunity to love and accept all that I am—just as I am. I learned how to take back the power to define who I am apart from certain opinions, outcomes, and circumstances that surround me in life. True inner freedom flows directly from my ability and choice to live from the inside out versus the outside in.

During my experience with cancer, another practice I started in the pursuit of inner freedom is transparency. Authentic transformation begins with valiant honesty and the ability to adjust. When I am confident enough to say, "This is who I am and I love who I am," I will not shrink back from the opportunity to express my feelings and insights. I will then be empowered to offer the same respect to others around me, without the need to own, control, and possess them.

Dating when I was bald and breastless was the most amazing opportunity to practice transparency and confidence. During this period, I went out on my first date with a man I'd had a huge crush on during freshman year of college.

During that date, as we sat side by side at the sushi bar, I remember thinking, *He is a great guy and I want another date, so I am going to lay it all out on the table.* I had shown up wearing my fake breasts and hot wig, but I looked straight ahead, took a deep breath, and told him, "I want you to know that one of my practices these days is transparency. Let me tell you a little about where I am on my journey. I have three kids, I got divorced over a year ago, I am going through stage three breast cancer, and I'm still in treatment. I'm bald and breastless, and I just want to know if this is a deal breaker for you?"

This single, hot, Greek man turned to me with his chocolate-brown eyes, thoughtfully surveying my wig as he finished his bite. He slowly shook his head as if to agree with what I said, and he spoke: "Hmm. Well, that is one sweet-looking wig. And don't worry about it—I'm a leg and butt man." After that, date number two—taking me to my ninth surgery—was on the calendar. Three years later, we walked down the aisle, and my children embraced him at our wedding. I believe that every storm produces beautiful rainbows in life; this was one of the big ones at the end of my storm.

Redefining my identity after going through cancer has led me into the practice of being curious and fascinated about all of life as it unfolds before me. I found that my expectations and assumptions as to how I felt life should be melted away in the light of expansive gratitude for the gift of each new day. I remember curiously seeking a way to shift the anxiety I felt going into chemo treatment into a positive experience. When I began to look at each treatment as an opportunity to connect with and encourage other people going through a similar situation, I was expanded by love. I resurrected my ability to live fearlessly and with a definitive purpose.

During treatment, I was graced with an out-of-body experience that deeply affected how I approached life. An out-of-body experience is when the soul leaves the body and is able to view the situation at hand from a place of observation and safety. Throughout my year of additional chemotherapy, I had to have periodic heart exams that involved injecting a dye into my heart. During one of these exams, my heart failed and I dropped to the ground. Instantly, my soul popped out of my body, and I witnessed from above several doctors and nurses frantically working on my body. I remember feeling expansive and weightless, able to tune into all feelings and details without any negative or oppressive emotions, actually feeling compassionate concern for the doctors' anxiety and wondering why they were so upset. When I dropped back into my body, I remember becoming aware of how heavy and restrictive it was, embarrassed for all of the moments I spent in fear, doubt, and worry.

Two questions remained within me after this experience, both of which grounded my sense of identity and personal success in life: One, how well did I love God, myself, and those around me? Two, how did I connect on a daily basis with my God-given talents and abilities and use them to inspire and bless those people around me? Each night before I fall asleep, I reflect on these questions, and ask others: Did I carve out time in my day to grow in my relationship with God? Linger in the wonderment of nature and relationships? Take time to nourish and exercise my body? Laugh? Practice living in gratitude? What actions did I take that reflect what I believe and value? I find that whatever I focus on before falling asleep reemerges the next day and affects how I see myself.

Cancer removed the veil of lies that I allowed myself to believe about what makes a woman beautiful and capable. I will never forget the moment I made the conscious commitment to love and accept myself, and embrace a conqueror's mind-set in spite of my circumstances and the image that I saw in the mirror. That bald and breastless reflection instantly revealed what I am and what I am not.

I never knew how attached I was to my hair and breasts until they were gone. Looking back now, it's easy to see that this loss was one of the greatest invitations into loving me within, no matter what I looked like on the outside. Today, I will often catch a glimpse of my scarred body before getting into the shower and I will pause, look myself in the eye, and say, "I love you! You made it through the storm and you are beautiful!"

We are women, beautiful, capable, confident women with or without hair, breasts, status, approval, recognition, or accomplishments. We are women...enough just as we are, infused with the ability to imagine the unimaginable, inspire the uninspired, motivate the unmotivated, and create the uncreated—all for a greater good on Earth.

Clare Munn is a premier leader in accelerating companies and connecting to social impact ventures. With more than twenty years of experience in starting and growing companies, her focus is on for-profit social impact companies and brands. Her expertise includes technology, global digital branding, marketing, partnership development, communications, sales, online publishing, and social media. In addition, Clare brings global expertise in mobile technology, business, and executive management to clients who are looking for scalable and lucrative digital strategies to find investment, sell, and/or sustain relevant audiences, quickly and effectively.

Clare is a cofounder and partner in GATE Global Impact, INC—concentrating on GATEwomen and GATEeducation. She is on the board of TCGAgency (The Communication Group), an award-winning digital advertising and social media agency she founded in 2004. TCG was one of the first fifty companies in San Francisco to be green certified and she connected all clients she worked with to a cause—clients such as eBay, AMD, Cisco, Hitachi, Chantecaille, McKesson, Danskin, 2(x)ist, OppenheimerFunds, Intuit, TheBullyMovie, and more. Clare is also a partner in SocMe Inc., a new start-up in test phase that is aimed at women 40 years or older, teaching them how to more happily and confidently navigate in the digital world we all now live in.

From a large publishing family, Clare was born and raised in Zimbabwe, and having lived in South Africa,

London, San Francisco, Los Angeles, and New York, she traversed the world of cultures, design, communication, and technology on a global scale. As a lifelong activist focused on women, children, family planning, education, health, and equality, Clare has served on boards and advisory boards of organizations such as Pangea Day, Artists for Literacy, Creative Visions, WomensHIVProgram, and We Advance, and has served as a trustee for Environment Africa and California Women's Conference. Clare's passion to educate and spread her knowledge of effective communication, emerging markets, and digital brand strategies has brought her in front of many audiences, including TED Women, The California Women's Conference, Fashion Forward, Adtech, West Coast Green, CNETNets, among others. She is currently writing a memoir, *African Moods*.

I grew up in Zimbabwe, where my father was one of the largest publishers in southern Africa. He had women on his board of directors forty-five years ago. So, as a young woman starting out, I didn't understand that women were supposed to think differently from men about what line of work they wanted to go into. One of my first "real" jobs was a summer internship with the Deputy Prime Minister of Britain; the Prime Minister then was Margaret Thatcher. It was after college that I started to observe differences. I became an intern for Lloyds of London in London and I recognized very quickly that maybe 1 percent of the workforce there was women.

One day, after having lunch in Trafalgar Square with Alexander, a colleague of mine of the same age, we went to deposit our paychecks. I happened to glance at his check and noticed the amount was at least 30 percent more than mine. I didn't think for a second that the inequality in pay had anything to do with the fact I was a woman. I just assumed it was a mistake. So I went to my boss and said to him, "Can you just fix this check? I don't know where the accounting department is." He looked at me, speechless, and then he fixed it.

A few years later, I realized what had actually transpired was that my lesser pay had not been a mistake but was on account of my being a woman. That's when I realized that I needed to speak up in these situations. I wished I had asked more questions of my boss so that I could have helped my female colleagues. I also learned that often the best way to correct this kind of situation isn't with aggression, but simply by asking questions. Of course, there were times when I was young when I was so eager to be noticed that I probably spoke up when I should have listened. As I got older, I learned that listening is a greater sign of wisdom and confidence—yet sometimes you have to speak out about gender inequality. If I sense in any shape or form an inequality in a room, it is rare that I don't speak out right away—often with wit, but there are times when I am fierce with my outrage.

118

Growing up in Zimbabwe probably gave me a different way of looking at things from most American women. I was born into an eccentric family. We thought television was absolutely diabolical, so we were voracious readers. And we lived in a multicultural society. I grew up blessed with different dialects, music, food, smells, and, above all, thoughts. This was in a period when southern Africa was going through an incredible transformation. Rhodesia didn't have an apartheid, but we did grow up in a war. I knew my family was privileged, but we also had the true gratitude that goes with understanding that you can lose anything at any moment. Also, because my father was a publisher, I was surrounded by creative and interesting global people all the time and they affected me tremendously. I am very grateful for that.

And of course, I've been blessed to have some special women in my life who have influenced who I am. My mother for one—a brilliant, eccentric, global person whose friends ranged from the country's most known artist to the chief of police, from gay hairdressers to Italian billionaires. All at the same table for lunch. This type of integration and acceptance led much of the way I still view the world. Then there was my nanny—an incredible, wonderful, regal woman with impeccable ethics. She was my parents' employee, but I never felt she was working for me; it felt more like I was working for her. She was a great influence on me.

My grandmother was involved with senior-home organizations. I recall going with her when I was a child. She would always say, "Remember, everyone has a story, and if they choose to share that with you, that is a privilege." Therefore, I never saw these "senior people" as anything but incredible storytellers. I would listen to them and ask them questions and learn the real power of storytelling, which influenced me in the line of work I chose and made me more effective as a communications professional.

Another woman who influenced me profoundly was the late Ruth Brinker. She started Project Open Hand in San Francisco in

1985 to deliver meals to people suffering from HIV/AIDS. (Project Open Hand now also serves people with other debilitating diseases, as well as the elderly.) Her next brainchild was Fresh Start Farms, a nonprofit that Ruth and I, along with Maria Pendergast and a few others, started in 1993. The concept was to employ and train homeless people in organic farming and to use rooftop spaces in the city for organic gardens. Unfortunately, San Francisco city laws didn't allow the ongoing vision of this organization, but I learned a lot about politics, powers of persuasion, and the underground truth of the homeless situation in San Francisco at that time from Ruth, who was a huge influence on my life.

And then there is Janet Padlad. She was a great producer at Paramount, who produced *Busy Town,* among other films. I met Janet when she bought the license to a story for TV, film, and video games. Our first phase was the video game, which I wrote for them at the age of twenty-four. This was my first deal in America. I remember vividly how direct and blunt she was in her speech, mannerisms, and overall energetic communication. She came across to me as hard, and I remember thinking that I didn't want to be like her, yet I knew it was a gift to learn how and why she had become successful. If she ever read this, she would laugh because she knows I came to respect her tremendously—partly because she is actually a marshmallow on the inside and because she was excellent at her work. At the time, though, the way she acted—as this very hard, masculine, driven character—affected me deeply.

I have been asked about what special contributions or viewpoints I bring to the workplace as a woman, but for me this again has as much to do with where I come from as what my gender is. I am a proud citizen of America now, but if I am in a room with mostly American-born men or women, I definitely bring something different, just as my American colleagues bring something different than me. I grew up pretty much blind to differences in gender, color, and age. I just *was*. But I suppose the generalizations people cite about differences between the sexes are valid.

Perhaps men tend to posture more and are more likely to laugh at themselves, while women tend to be more empathetic and also to beat up on themselves. But I know how to bring laughter to a room—usually by laughing at myself. It lights up the room and, I suppose, helps give me an opening.

If it is true that women can multitask or think in a more resourceful way, then I am happy to be female, because in my business you have to juggle a lot of balls at once. If you don't think things through differently and creatively, then you don't stand out as a strategist, so I'm happy to be a woman in my line of work. However, I find that women can be a pain in the arse too. We are such codependent creatures sometimes, and it is often a relief to be with a bunch of dudes who want to get one thing done and move onto the next without having to have a democratic revolution. It really is the balance, and when we strike that balance, that is when and where "equality" will reign. There are so many amazing men, and I look to them to move the needle now. And I look to women to help mentor other women/girls to learn from their mistakes and best practices. I have great hope this is happening and will continue to in a much broader way. I watch my partner's thirteen-year-old son and his friends of all genders and colors and backgrounds, and all I see is camaraderie. Yes, I have great hope.

Men and women do tend to behave differently, but there are many exceptions to the stereotypes. I know many men who are as sensitive as, or more so than, women typically are thought to be. I have an ego, but the way I handle it is sometimes different. I know that I think differently when I am in a room full of men. I don't mean I think more intelligently, just differently, and there is value in that. It's a gross generalization, but yes, I do think that women think differently.

And I do think there are areas where we need to be activists, pushing for global equal rights. It is no secret that companies that have women on their boards do better. Numerous articles support this. I certainly believe that when there is a balance of estrogen and testosterone in the room, it is an easier place to be. But the big issues for me are unequal pay, more executive job opportunities, and a larger representation of women on corporate boards.

Also, there are things we can each do in our everyday lives to help this initiative of equal rights. For instance, when you have to choose a doctor from your insurance company's network, look at the rankings and make some calls about the female doctors and if it all looks right, choose a female over a male where possible. Likewise, find out the café in your area that is owned by a woman and if the service and food is up to your standards, frequent that spot versus a corporate franchise. These might be small things to some, but I think they are good and easy check marks to consider and do. Also, mentor other women as much as you possibly can, and don't forget about yourself; make sure you have a mentor of your own. We all get so busy that we forget that there are always wiser people out there who can help us, which in turn allows us more time to help others.

And finally, use social media. LinkedIn is wonderful. I do a lot of training on how to use different platforms. One thing I stress is that before you do your profile or edit it, stop and think through what you are aspiring to be in the next year, the next three years. Do you know yourself well enough? Then go find a person who is doing the job to which you aspire and find out how that woman got there and what her journey was like.

Writing your profile is an exercise in giving yourself a brand. And in a way it is a meditation. I am big on meditation. It is a godsend just to quiet my mind, even if it is only five to fifteen minutes a day. It is just a beautiful thing to do. And if you can't get into meditation, even taking fifteen minutes for a walk or listening to music can help quiet your mind and help you to find out if your daily purpose or intention is being met. When we aren't meeting our daily purpose, it's most likely because we're going down too many different paths that we haven't really thought through. Believe you me, this is something I have to consider daily and drives my PAs bananas. My ADHD doesn't help matters, yet in a way, it has ensured that I have structures in place to keep on track.

As a storyteller and producer, I feel very privileged to do what I do, because I get to learn from the decision makers in some great organizations. I'm learning about the innermost vulnerable aspects of a company and its leaders, and to do that well requires a positive form of manipulation. You have to manipulate, in the sense of getting the truth out of somebody. I don't mean that we manipulate the truth once we have the facts, but you have to "do the dance" in order to get the information you need to do your job for your client—and do so as transparently and as gently as possible. The term "manipulation" has a bad connotation in this country, but it is an honest term. We all do it every day of our lives.

I'd like to end here by suggesting we all be gentle on ourselves too. We are inundated with information, life, and transitions of all forms. Beating ourselves up isn't going to help, and being angry toward the world, men, or anyone for that matter, doesn't ever help in my opinion. Try and find ways to daily celebrate something—perhaps starting with you.

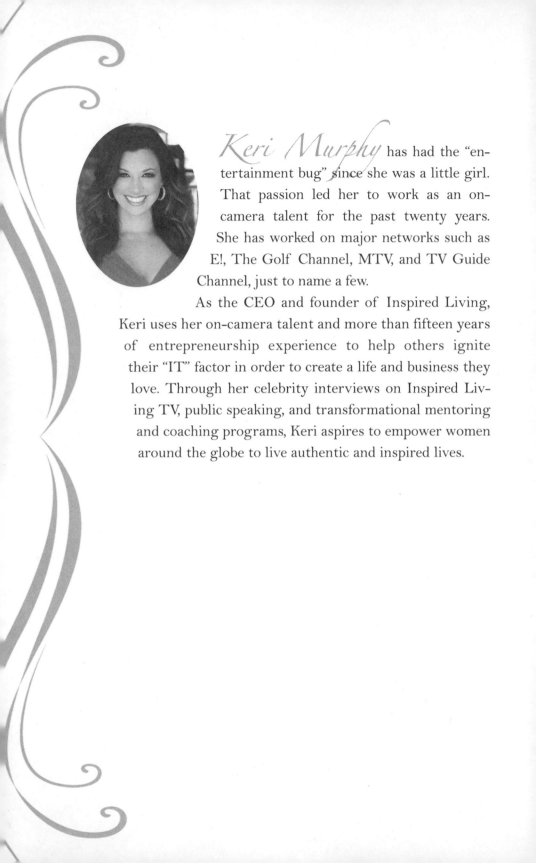

Keri Murphy has had the "entertainment bug" since she was a little girl. That passion led her to work as an on-camera talent for the past twenty years. She has worked on major networks such as E!, The Golf Channel, MTV, and TV Guide Channel, just to name a few.

As the CEO and founder of Inspired Living, Keri uses her on-camera talent and more than fifteen years of entrepreneurship experience to help others ignite their "IT" factor in order to create a life and business they love. Through her celebrity interviews on Inspired Living TV, public speaking, and transformational mentoring and coaching programs, Keri aspires to empower women around the globe to live authentic and inspired lives.

Some people have "jobs" they go to every day, and some people build their careers around something they are truly called to do. I'm fortunate to be in that second category. Inspired Living is my life and my passion. There is no separation between me as a person and the work I do, inspiring people to live the lives they were called to. This is who I am. Although I have been an entrepreneur for many years, it wasn't until I lost everything and was forced to start over that I can now truly say that I am an entrepreneur.

This is a great time for women. Things are significantly better for women in business than they were as little as ten years ago. There is a global shift taking place; part of that is women feeling free to ask for help in building their businesses. I think that for too long we were trying to do it alone. I know I did! In some ways, it is still kind of a man's world, and we still have to go out there and prove ourselves. But there has never been a better time to do that.

There is a lot of opportunity for women in business today, and it shows in the statistics on start-ups. I love being a woman in business; I couldn't imagine being anything else. Some of us still feel that there are limitations on how far we can go because we aren't men and can't get the support we need, but I think those limitations are vanishing. I think we are going to see more and more women stepping into their greatness and building multimillion-dollar businesses.

I never think about whether I should do something one way or another on account of being a woman. But there are certainly differences between women and men in the way we function. My partner and amazing "other half" is also an entrepreneur. We are very different when it comes to business and in the way we communicate with each other. Men seem to need to claim their territories, to prove themselves. They want to rationalize things with facts and statistics. I don't feel a constant need to go out and prove myself. I just talk

125

about what I am passionate about and what I know. Women speak more from the heart than from the head. So it's important to be who we are, to use our heart and intuition. When we speak from that place, people are more drawn to us. I call that having the "IT" factor! It means being truly authentic to who you are.

So it's a big factor in my success that I never try to be a man. My success has come from my heart and from collaborating with other women (collaboration is another thing women are good at). Two other components of my success are being true to my calling and not getting stuck in the minutia of running the business. My gift is the ability to go out and share my business and passion with others, to help others see what they are capable of creating in their lives regardless of circumstances. Knowing your strong suit is very important. One of my mentors said to me, "Keri, you should always be functioning at your best and highest use possible." I think of that regularly and make sure I delegate the things that I am not good at.

Of course, sometimes our strengths can be our weaknesses, too. Sometimes women are so heart-focused that we don't pay enough attention to the financial or organizational side. We don't get the necessary systems and operations in place. I now have those systems in place because I hired the right people to make it happen. And I don't hire people just because I like them. I want to hire people who are better than I am. Men are really great at hiring the right people, but there is a sort of boys' club where they take care of each other. I think women can gain a lot by doing that. We have this talent for collaborating, but we also tend to look with envy at other women who are successful, rather than find out how they did it. We need to stop competing and start collaborating more; there is plenty of business and people out there for all of us!

The number one contributor to my success is my faith in God, in something that is bigger than I am. I do not believe our dreams and aspirations are an accident. I believe we all are given gifts that we are supposed to share with the world. Not doing so is an injustice to our maker, ourselves, and the world around us.

The next most important factor is something I learned in defeat. I had to close a company that I loved when the recession hit in 2008. However, it wasn't just the recession. I never had a mentor or group of other successful women to turn to. I also didn't have a long-term financial strategy or the right financial systems in place, including a forecasting system. I filed for bankruptcy in 2008, sold my house as a short sale, packed up my car, and moved to Los Angeles.

Ever since I was a little girl, I knew I wanted to be a speaker and perform on camera. I knew I could do this, but I had always put that desire in a box and set it aside. I opened that box once in a while when I hosted events or worked on-camera, but I'd close it up again and put it on a shelf, thinking, *Maybe later.* So when I closed my business, I had nothing left but to open that box. That was when I gave myself permission to do what I knew I was called to do. My new business grew to provide me a six-figure income in less than two years. That didn't happen because I knew it all. It happened because I was doing what I was called to do, but I had never had the belief I could do it full time and make a great income.

I remember the moment I understood what I had to do. I was in a casting office with at least 200 other women auditioning for a $15,000 job. I waited three hours to get two minutes to prove that I was good enough for this job. I knew I could do it. I had worked on television networks from E! to The Golf Channel. Being on camera was my thing. It seemed absurd that I was going to have just two minutes to get someone to validate me, to tell me I deserved that job. That was the moment the light switched on. I told myself I was no longer going to put off or ask for permission to do what I knew I was supposed to do; now, that is what I share with others. We shouldn't wait for someone to validate our dreams.

Shortly after that, I launched Inspired Living and I started coaching people on how to build businesses around their natural gifts.

I started helping people around the globe realize their potential and ignite their "IT" factor. I realized how important it is to trust your intuition and follow your passion. In order to help people see they were not alone in their quest, I started interviewing celebrities about how they got where they are today. I love sharing these stories because it shows that no level of success is accomplished without overcoming challenges. My first interview was with the star of *Hercules*, Kevin Sorbo. People ask me how I get celebrities to sit down for an interview with me. The answer: I ask them. I no longer wait for permission. And that is how Inspired Living took off.

I know for many women it is easy just to keep going to work rather than to go out and do what they are called to do. But making a big life decision from the heart is what transforms women's lives. It's how I started Inspired Living, and it's what Inspired Living teaches the women who come to us. When we are inspired . . . we inspire others!

Women bring so many special qualities to the business world, including empathy and sensitivity. I think being emotional, and being able to share our emotions, is a gift. We can be open and vulnerable in business and still be strong. Men still seem to feel that they always have to be strong—that they can't let people see their weaknesses or the areas where they lack knowledge. Women can let that guard down, drop the façade. And we can share our triumphs and challenges with each other. I love being a woman in business because I can turn to my women colleagues and friends. I think that's amazing.

Here's an example. At a training session in London, I met a woman, Michele, who had been an accountant for thirty years. In a breakout session, she spoke in a way that reached into my heart and soul. Afterward, she told me that was the first time she had spoken in any public arena. I have worked with her for two years, and she has become very successful in her coaching and speaking business. That truly inspires me, and Michele is out there inspiring other women to change their lives. It's never too late!

My business is about helping women realize who they want to BE in this world and the life they want to (and can) create. But there are ways in which all successful women can and should help others do this. You can be part of an organization like the Women Network and be a mentor to someone who is new to business. I am currently a mentor to two young entrepreneurs in Jamaica through the Branson Centre of Entrepreneurship and I get so much from working with them. You can also write articles, give to underserved women in your community, or give your time, money, or talents.

You get what you give. It doesn't have to be a lot. Giving back is sharing the energy of the universe, and I think it is imperative to your long-term success. Most of the entrepreneurs I work with who have reached $1 million are very big on giving back. But you don't have to be an entrepreneur to help other women build their businesses.

There are many ways you can help yourself as well. First and foremost, believe in yourself. Next, listen to that voice inside your soul that keeps nagging you to do what you are called to do. That is a divine gift. Our dreams are not accidents. We are not given these visions and desires without the resources to make them reality.

Here's the thing, though: You have to be willing to be uncomfortable. You have to be willing to take the steps that are needed to bring your visions to life. Get out of your comfort zone. Too many of us go right back to what we know, to where we're comfortable, the minute we feel resistance or insecurity. That is why only 6 percent of Americans are making more than $100,000 a year. It's not that they aren't smart enough; it is because they are not willing to do what it takes.

I teach people to work on my four Ds: Decide, Dedicate, Develop, and Deliver. How are you doing those four things in your life? Have you even decided what you want to do in your life? You have to get clear on what it is that you want to create. You have to make the decision and then dedicate yourself. Perseverance and tenacity are the differences between those who want something and those who achieve it. You have to be developing always. The minute you think you know everything is when you think you know your limit. So always keep developing yourself so you can deliver your voice, your talent to the world. Dream it. Live it. BE it!

Monique Nadeau is the founder of Grow Your Family Strong, a new venture helping families to elevate nutrition through technology and practical tools. She is also a cofounder and board member of Hope Street Group, a national public policy organization dedicated to solving our nation's critical jobs, health care, and education issues.

Monique was an investment banker for more than fourteen years in London, Paris, and New York. She was the youngest managing director globally at Dresdner Kleinwort Wasserstein, pioneering more than $4 billion of public-private finance initiatives for the UK government and advising public and private institutions about high-profile strategic risk management transactions. She has an MPA from Harvard University and has traveled and worked extensively abroad.

When it comes to success, be it personal or professional, I don't believe there are any traits that are inherently based on whether one is biologically female or male. In fact, I don't believe that there is any success a man can achieve that a woman cannot and vice versa.

Success can have many meanings to different people. Yet I believe there are some core tenets that are common to all types of success:

- **Work hard.** There's no doubt that hard work is essential. You could be lucky, but I really believe that the harder you work, the luckier you get, so it's better to work hard. You need long-term goals, whether small or large, to give that hard work purpose and direction. But remember that it's highly unlikely that the plan you made at the outset to reach those goals will ever be what you end up doing to achieve them. Some things won't happen; unexpected things will. So you have to have an ability to adapt to different situations and roll with the punches. Success is as much about sticking to your goals as it is about bright ideas.
- **Find people that believe in you and are willing to give you a chance.** Although it's not essential to success, there's no doubt that a strong support network makes things easier. For me, these people—family, friends, mentors, and associates—care enough to give me both constructive criticism and praise when I need it. It can be really hard to focus on the people you meet as part of your journey to success, but it helps to be curious about them and engage with them. I'm fortunate, because I find people naturally interesting, and that fascination has built numerous serendipitous relationships and friendships that, although unplanned, were instrumental to my success.

- **For women specifically: Incrementally stretch beyond your comfort zone**. I've found that we support each other best when we give each other increasing opportunities to prove ourselves. Yet, unlike many men, women don't tend to jump into assignments where we have little knowledge or experience. We need to engage with them in increments and benefit from a lot of encouragement along the way.

- **Be bolder and encourage boldness in those around you.** First, applaud ambition. Second, and more important, do not dwell on failure. By this, I don't mean to disregard missteps. You're not living if you don't make some mistakes along the way. I think women in particular get hung up on failure.

- **Take advantage of opportunities to help.** Whether it's time, advice, support, money, or a million other things, there are always ways to help or pay it forward. In turn, if you receive the benefit of this kind of supportive relationship, make the most of it and be grateful.

- **Be direct and honest**. Specific and actionable feedback is the most powerful tool to understand failure and find success. Success doesn't care about kindness or hurt feelings. It only cares about being better and doing better. Women really help each other by ensuring that we tell it as it is to each other.

- **Tap into your passion.** I've met and been impressed with a lot of women in many different areas, including women I've met in politics. I've been a big fan of Barbara Mikulski, the senior senator from Maryland, and the longest-serving woman in the history of Congress. What I love most about her is that she entered politics because of her passion and activism for justice, equality, and opportunity for all Americans, and she has stood for that every day she's been in office. Her achievements and success are remarkable, and though she's tiny in stature, her influence and people's respect for her are massive.

And finally:

- **Focus on what supports success.** If you can deliver and build relationships and allies around you, you can succeed. If you stick to substance, you can succeed. (One of my mentors, Julie Morgenstern—an internationally renowned organizing and time management expert, and a *New York Times* bestselling author, consultant, and speaker—has always said to me that there is security in substance. She's absolutely right. Ifs, buts, and maybes don't lead to success—stick to the facts.) If you commit completely to a goal but not a specific plan, you can succeed. That said, the world is not perfect! Don't be afraid to ask for equality and if you don't get it, demand it. I believe in supporting meritocracy where everybody should have the opportunity to compete to the best of their abilities.

Janice Neiderhofer, MA, PhDc, is the innovative creator and president of Elite Spy Adventures (ESA), designed to empower people through experience. ESA offers unique and customized events designed to draw out new levels of strength and confidence through careful motivation during physically, mentally, and psychologically exacting challenges. Janice is uniquely qualified to develop these unparalleled programs, with decades of training and experience earned in her outstanding career in law enforcement. In her early years she was a police officer with two departments, then served a distinguished twenty-one-year career with the Drug Enforcement Administration (DEA)—the single-mission US federal agency with a reputation as the world's premier drug enforcement organization.

As an elite member of internationally recognized law enforcement teams, Janice received incomparable training, serving as an undercover agent, SWAT team member, police hostage negotiator, interviewer/interrogator, and body language expert, which earned her status as a master communicator and expert in leadership development. As a subject-matter expert, she has taught these skills in numerous programs to all levels of law enforcement agencies, including the DEA, FBI, Secret Service, CIA, ATF, and the Department of Homeland Security.

Since retiring from the DEA, Janice has been in demand by global clients as a consulting advisor and speaker. She is a powerhouse talent with degrees in psychology, criminal justice, and forensic psychophysiology, and she combines her expansive knowledge and extraordinary life experience with a passion to empower others to get on target to reach their potential. She uses well-honed skills and transformative insight to guide students through mind-stretching challenges that develop leadership strength. Her team-building programs have delivered success for executives, entrepreneurs, and high-ranking members of law enforcement agencies worldwide. Janice's programs have been featured on network and cable television for their unique concepts and proven success.

The sun shone into the driver's door window of my patrol car on a seemingly calm Sunday afternoon. I had parked across the way from George, a badass police officer who had venom coursing through his veins for women who carried a badge and gun. He had responded to a "kid call" from dispatch, which meant kids were disturbing the neighborhood.

I was a shrewd cop and knew the neighborhood in which George's call was located had a reputation for violence. I sat in my car, working on paperwork, just in case things took a turn for the worse.

George's voice came screeching over the police radio requesting immediate cover. I looked at the radio in disbelief and it took only a few seconds for me to register that the indestructible George was in trouble.

"Seven Adam thirty-one, I'm here," I responded back into the radio and swooped in to help.

George was in a physical confrontation with a suspect equal to his slender six foot five frame. I quickly assessed the situation. George was holding his own against the suspect. I noticed a man of equal height but who weighed upward of 400 pounds making his way toward George and his suspect.

He walked like a slow-moving freight train and slurred, "That's my brother, that's my brother." He had his sights on saving his brother from George. He didn't even notice me directly in front of him, ordering him to stop—he just kept advancing.

I poked him three times in the middle of his chest with my finger, desperately attempting to gain his attention. He glanced down at me as if I were nothing but a fly bothering him. He looked over my head at his brother and kept pressing onward. I knew that if this massive man made his way to his brother and George, who was fighting for his life, things would turn deadly.

I scrambled behind him and jumped up three times to gain enough height to secure my arm around his thick neck. Applying a chokehold, I swept his feet out from under him and pinned him to the ground.

George had succeeded in getting his suspect handcuffed and se-cured in the back seat of his patrol car. I could hear an angry crowd funneling out of the adjacent apartments. George came running over and asked if I was okay.

"F*&% no! Handcuff him!" was my response, and I held him in place while George shackled his hands behind his back.

I could hear sirens in the distance coming to our aid, but they seemed too far away. As George and I were getting the man to his feet, the suspect in the back of the patrol car kicked out the window and attempted to escape. The angry crowd was drawing down upon us.

George and I sat in a small, dingy, gray room at police headquar-ters, writing our reports as we silently contemplated how lucky we were that backup had arrived in time. But I still felt like a cornered animal, knowing all too well George's opinion of female police offi-cers. I desperately wanted to escape the thick, dark air of contempt.

Without lifting his head from his report, George broke the un-comfortable silence. "Do you want to get something to eat?"

Surprised, I decided there must be only one correct answer. "Yes?"

Our separate patrol cars were parked outside the restaurant. We sat across from each other in a booth, wrapped in all too familiar tense silence. George held his hamburger in both hands, looking down, when suddenly he peered up at me and announced, "I never thought I'd say this, but you were the best f*%&ing cover I ever had."

I hadn't consciously intended to break the glass ceiling, but I realized that *we all must recognize when we are being called to do great-ness in the world and get out of our own way.* It is my calling to be in the service of humanity and the greater good.

I was born outside of Detroit, Michigan, and grew up with my four brothers and my parents. I was the only girl and the fourth born. My childhood was one peppered with violence and chaos, a battleground of physical and psychological abuse. Nurturing, proper touch, and obvious love were foreign concepts. Normal conversa-tions were fleeting. There was only screaming and yelling. I don't remember laughing or playing, only enduring.

Because of this, I learned early how to read people, their body language, voices, language patterns, and emotions. I knew what they were going to do even before they did. I was capable of quickly and effectively adjusting to my environment and the people in it. I was often able to skirt violence and danger. I never felt like a child. It was as if I had been born an adult, having to think and act like one. And so wisdom came early, as well as a wealth of common sense. In my early years, I became a problem solver and an adrenaline junkie.

During my junior year of college, my criminal justice professor made an announcement: "If you think you're so smart and want to be police officers, go to Ocean City, Maryland, for the summer. They hire sixty extra seasonal officers, train you during a short police academy, and put you out on the streets by yourself with a gun!" Five of us piled in a car and drove from Michigan State University all the way to Ocean City, Maryland. We were interviewed and hired.

That summer between my junior and senior years of college was my first taste of working in law enforcement. Up until this point, my plan had been to attend law school, which, once accomplished, would be proof of my intelligence and wealth—two things I didn't have as a kid. But destiny had a different plan for me.

Once I was sworn in as a police officer, intoxicating experiences kept coming. I was issued a six-shot revolver, a badge, a uniform, and a shiny patrol car. I was patrolling the city—*alone*! Right from the start, I tasted my first undercover drug work. The police department asked me to work undercover on what would have been my days off. Working undercover gave me permission to be someone else— someone other than the brutally shy and invisible girl from Detroit.

A common law enforcement saying—*once you get it in your blood, you can't get it out*—proved true. I was hooked!

My innate skills served me well. I could read people; I knew their needs, what drove them. And I used this to my advantage. Undercover work ran through my veins. By putting my life in danger, I felt assured that I was working in the service of others.

During my formative years, I subconsciously learned the false truth that men were the stronger sex, and so acquired many classic traits of men: physically strong, competitive, decisive, independent, focused, unstoppable. Because of this, I felt weirdly comfortable in the traditionally male world of law enforcement.

Survival was the name of my game and existing like a man meant I could take care of myself and at the same time save the world. I believed law enforcement was a calling just like the calling of a priest or nun. I believed I did not have a choice—I had to serve my country and humankind.

Even so, I never characterized myself as taking on a male persona. After the execution of a search and/or arrest warrant, kicking down a door, holding a submachine gun, strapped in raid gear, the following day I'd wear a dress to the office, believing I was being feminine. I was proving a point that women could do the job as well as or better than my male counterparts. It was my way of saying, "In your *face*."

I didn't realize I was far from being feminine. I had no clue that people could not see my big heart, giving nature, or natural desire for love. What they saw was a bold, smart, independent, invincible machine who required no help from anyone.

Despite my firsthand knowledge of the difficulties women police officers face and instead of developing solidarity with my female colleagues, women became my biggest competition during my career at a second police department. What contributed to this competition was when a new male recruit came on the job, the seasoned guys would take him out and test him, which usually meant getting into a physical altercation. If he held his own and won the fight, then he was accepted throughout the ranks.

This standard was not the same for women. With every new male partner a woman worked with, she had to prove herself again. She was tested each and every time to see if she could be trusted in life-threatening situations. It was a constant battleground and a woman had to be sharp, courageous, and determined at every moment.

This made women my targets. If they were weak, complained, flirted, or didn't hold their own, I detested them. And since I had grown up with all boys, I really did not know how to relate to women. I had earned my stake in the world as strong, independent, and equal to men. But I would soon discover yet another facet of my chosen career: what it meant to be a target for workplace sexism.

In the history of the police department, never had a woman been assigned to the elite narcotics unit. As the police department's golden girl, I was considered the best of the best and was frequently assigned to what were considered "badass" assignments, customarily for the male crème de la crème. I was often asked to work undercover, everything from posing as a decoy for a stalker to prostitute detail to buying and selling illegal narcotics.

It was forbidden for a woman to be in the narcotics unit on a full-time basis, but it was acceptable to my male counterparts for me to participate as long as I was on loan from patrol for a special detail.

When a position in the detective bureau opened, I didn't hesitate to apply. It was the next best thing to the narcotics unit. I completed the selection process and was ranked number one. This assured me a position. A week later, an opening for the narcotics unit was advertised. Much to everyone's surprise, I applied, tested, and was ranked number one once again. (I suspected that the department attempted to time the openings in an effort to get me into the detective bureau, where women were more accepted.)

After applying for the positions, I was still working in the patrol unit awaiting my transfer to narcotics. There had been a rumor circulating around the police department that the only way I could have possibly been ranked number one for both the detective bureau and the narcotics unit was to have slept with the police captain. The men needed so badly to believe that I could not have earned these positions on my own merit.

One day I was standing in police headquarters in uniform when my patrol sector partner walked in. We had been in many life and death situations on the streets together, we knew each other well, and trust had been long established. After sauntering toward me he stopped, and with disdain looked me up and down. He said nothing, but the message was clear, and my heart sank.

"You too?" I asked. Even my own sector partner believed the vicious rumor.

After he walked off, I stood there in disbelief. I thought, *This has got to be the worst it can get. If I can't handle this, then I better get out of law enforcement.* In the end, though, I stayed the course—although my path shifted slightly.

My first positive mentors, the supervisors in the narcotics unit, convinced me that I should not waste away in a thirty-year career in a local police department. Their advice: "Go federal."

I was a highly qualified applicant for the FBI and DEA, and they pursued me as if I were a prizefighter because of my experience. I applied at both agencies, and they offered me a special agent position at the same time.

The FBI informed me that their policy wouldn't allow me to work undercover for seven years. My response: "If you think I am going to push a pencil and paper for seven years, you're wrong." I chose the DEA and off I went to complete the academy in Quantico, Virginia.

My first assignment out of the academy was in Denver, Colorado. My undercover work experience paid off the first week as a special agent, and my first narcotics case was one of the largest the office had ever seen.

I was excited to return from the streets to the DEA office Monday morning with amazing results in tow. To my disbelief, my fellow agents looked at me as if I had done something wrong!

Their obvious jealousy prompted me to call an old comrade, a narcotics detective who was still working at my former police department. I asked if he would accompany me to a meeting with the new chief of police to ask for my old position back.

We sat across the imposing desk of the chief of police and, after I disclosed my desire to return to the police department, he simply asked, "Why would you want to? Oh, don't get me wrong, I may not know you, but I know *of* you. And I would take you back in a heartbeat. But you are now a *federal agent!*" Hearing that voice of wisdom, I put my tail between my legs and returned to the DEA.

While working as a street agent at the DEA, I also became the second and youngest female firearms and tactical instructor. I was in charge of a large division inclusive of a four-state area. I designed a one-of-a-kind program that further built my reputation as a ceiling breaker.

I had an arsenal of life lessons and became even more effective at influencing people. I spoke to anyone, anywhere, anytime under any circumstance. I became an interviewer and interrogator for the DEA and traveled the world. I earned the nickname "the Terminator" because I could easily build trust with suspects and obtain written, signed, and dated confessions.

Armed with my human behavior skills, my goal was to affect criminals' lives in positive ways, and many times they thanked me for changing their lives, all the while still giving me the desired confession. My top-secret weapons? Honor and respect.

Many suspects had never been shown honor or respect. I knew that these men and women weren't born criminals. There are many, many reasons why a person turns to a life of crime. It was up to me to get curious as to why they ended up where they were.

It is the choices we make or don't make that lead us down our paths. Sometimes, we don't even know that there are other choices until they are pointed out or taught to us. Growing up where I did, I could have easily made the wrong choices and ended up just like them, lost. Because of this, I am a strong advocate for stepping into the mentor role and supporting others, especially women. When you teach a man, you have educated a man. But when you teach a woman, you have educated a whole community.

I was not satisfied just being a special agent, so I decided to bring all the human behavior tools, skills, and strategies to the world of law enforcement, and under the DEA's watchful eye I began to teach. I used my expertise in interviewing and interrogation as an opportunity to influence transformation in the men and women behind the badge. I was in high demand and taught at the Central Intelligence Agency (CIA); Federal Bureau of Investigation (FBI); Drug Enforcement Administration (DEA); Secret Service (SS); Alcohol, Tobacco, & Firearms (ATF); Homeland Security (HS); US Immigration and Customs Enforcement (ICE); and the American Polygraph Association (APA), and was an adjunct instructor for the DEA Academy and for the Department of Defense, to mention just a few.

But after twenty-nine years, the law enforcement world had taken its toll on me, and I was eager and determined to complete that part of my life and get to retirement. I was leaving a lot of blood, sweat, and tears behind and I wanted a psychological payoff for all of my accomplishments.

I retired at the earliest allowable age. My intention was to go out and immediately spread my wings in the real world.

Today, I am in the spring of my life. Now that I've left the world of law enforcement, I created Elite Spy Adventures, a program designed to empower women and men through one-of-a-kind spy adventures. I get to share my vast toolbox of life lessons, skills, tools, and strategies for a worthy cause: influencing people to change their lives.

Every one of us is on our own hero's journey and that story defines us. But your story can also keep you from greatness, from owning your power and allowing your gift of womanhood to shine naturally. If you do not recognize the purpose of your own hero's journey, its true meaning will be lost. The lessons learned will never be discovered and shared with others.

Each woman has the opportunity to decide how her journey will be defined. When she lives in her feminine power, when she honors not only where she wants to go but where she's been, she will find peace as well as the success each of us desires and deserves.

Yesterday is a lesson. Today is an opportunity. Tomorrow is a gift.

Sophia A. Nelson, Esq., is an American award-winning author, former White House correspondent, television personality, and the *Huffington Post's* Healthy Living, Women & Business columnist. Sophia appears regularly on MSNBC as a contributor and TV ONE analyst. She has appeared on numerous other networks and television shows such as the BBC, CNN, FOX, C-Span, the *Today Show, Nightly News with Diane Sawyer*, and more as a political and cultural expert, thought leader, and attorney, covering many topics of national and global interest.

Sophia is the author of the award-winning 2011 nonfiction book *Black Woman Redefined: Dispelling Myths and Discovering Fulfillment in the Age of Michelle Obama*. Sophia is a highly sought-after motivational speaker and leadership trainer for Fortune 500 companies, as well as universities. She writes a national lifestyle and political column for *Newsweek's The Daily Beast*, and is a frequent contributor to *USA Today, Essence Magazine*, and the *Washington Post*. Her second book, *The Woman Code: 20 Powerful Keys to Unlock Your Life* (Revell), is due out in stores worldwide October 2014.

Madeline Albright, former US Secretary of State, said it best: "There is a very special place in hell for women that don't help other women." These are powerful and important words. As a black woman professional, one of the things that I see consistently that has me deeply concerned about women in our modern culture is this attitude of competition versus collaboration.

Although men are competitors (and fierce ones at that), they also know how to be fierce collaborators. They know how to get on the golf course, sit in the bar, put on the boxing gloves, play racquetball, work on their business deals, and figure out how they can come together and make deals and dollars. As women, we often miss the mark. Many of us will sit around and tear one another down, and say "I don't like," "I heard," and "she did" instead of finding a way to collaborate with each other to build up one another and succeed.

There is a code, a woman code. That's the name of my second book and I bring this up intentionally, not to promote a book, but to prove a point: It matters how we live, how we work, and how we play. There are certain roads of living in the spirit of who we are supposed to be as human beings that we should not violate. The women I admire and the women that I know who are successful honor the woman code. They are collaborators. They don't talk bad about other women. They don't tear other women down. They don't gossip. They don't demean other women. They are too busy being successful for that kind of nonsense, and they don't have time for it. Successful women cultivate and collaborate, and in doing so, they create success.

I entered the field of journalism after transitioning from a ten-year career as an attorney. There are many more women in journalism now than when I first came to Washington, DC, as a high school student and later, in the late 1980s, as a college student. Women journalists like Cokie Roberts, the late Helen Thomas, and Andrea

Mitchell have done spectacular things to take journalism to another level. And while women's influence in the media is enormous now, I would like to see more women owners running media outlets as opposed to what it is now: a very homogenous group of white males with women in more subordinate, subsidiary-type roles. You have women like Arianna Huffington and Tina Brown, owners of Huffington Post Media and Daily Beast, respectively, who are changing this paradigm. However, it's been noted in such publications as the *Wall Street Journal* and *Forbes* that women just don't have the capital to own major media outlets. And owners of media-related entities can directly influence what images are seen of women, either positive or negative.

Likewise, there are still things we as women cannot do in the workplace. For instance, we cannot get "upset" in a meeting the same way a man can. We can't throw papers across the table when we are frustrated or curse as men do. When a man shows emotion in the workplace, it's seen as him just letting off steam, but for women, such behavior would be a career-limiting move at best and most likely career ending. A woman displaying emotion in the workplace is perceived as having anger management issues. I think most women who are successful know how to play the game while still being strong, smart, and intelligent and having their say and navigating in a way that allows them neither to put men off nor have men see them as a threat or as overly assertive.

Women bring a different perspective and a range of unique experiences, which is a great thing. For me, my mother and my family were pivotal influences on my personal success. My mother worked as a nurse and sacrificed much for her children. She made me the woman that I am today. I know that I wouldn't be who I am today without the encouragement, sponsorship, and mentoring from the women who have been essential in my life.

Although I think that talent is gender neutral, women have a different way of looking at things and handling them. I also know that as a black woman, my interactions with others are sometimes based on my context (i.e., being a woman of color). My hunch is that the first thing people see of me, and women who look like me, is my race, not my gender. This can be a mixed bag of blessings and curses. I, like millions of other women of color, have learned to be comfortable being the "only one" in the room if need be, but I am hopeful that a day will come that we will all be comfortable in the same room, regardless of what that room's demographic makeup happens to be!

In the final analysis, we as women are often our own worst enemies and if we can learn to unlock our internal code, we can become our own best friends. We as a sisterhood of women must commit to ridding the workplace of those queen bee–types who feel the need to haze other women because they were hazed. We need to teach women how to get along and lift one another as we climb. We need to get back to our code. It is your obligation and your responsibility as a woman to help other women. It isn't about whether you like the person or feel you know what's right for her. Instead, if you see talent and ability, be a mentor or a sponsor and work to nurture those traits the same way someone did for you. Why would another woman expect to have success in her career thanks to the help of others, and yet not feel that she has to help pass it forward?

That's not cool, and that's not code. Sisters, it's time for the universal one woman to emerge. You are your sister's keeper. It's time to put the "sister" back in sisterhood.

Carolyn Parks is publisher of SlowStruck.com, an engaging online lifestyle magazine promoting the philosophy that "taking time is the ultimate rush." Formerly, Carolyn was founder of Outstanding Women Speakers, a North American all-women speakers bureau. She is proud to be an advisory board member for The Women Network, a visionary organization dedicated to empowering women internationally.

Years ago, when I was an entrepreneur producing a women's consumer show and booking speakers, I was surprised to learn that significantly more men than women were being promoted as professional speakers. The ratio was approximately four to one in favor of men.

It struck me like a lightning bolt that this ratio was unrealistic in terms of reflecting the true pool of talent out there. It doesn't take a genius to conclude that inspiration comes from all of humanity, not just men. I saw a disparity and wanted to address it. I was immediately inspired to launch an all-women speakers bureau; I was not only attracted to the speaking industry because of my events background and my own love of public speaking but also because I truly wanted to level the playing field. Women working alongside talented men, offering the world inspiration and knowledge—that's the way it should be!

Skip ahead some years and the ratio has definitely changed for the better. Women are being recognized and promoted in abundance, but women speakers are still sorely needed as role models in certain areas of business, technology, science, and manufacturing. As more women take the helm in these sectors—and they are doing so!—the key is to encourage them to get out there in the public arena and share their messages. Organizations like TED are doing wonders to achieve this goal.

Every individual offers unique gifts. I believe that we should focus on what humanity can achieve together through appreciating each person's unique gifts—gender aside. But (there's that proverbial "but"!) I believe that there are some general traits more closely associated with how women express their knowledge and talents than with how men do. And if my observations are based on reality, it just affirms for me that great things can happen when men and women work together, through the blending and acceptance of these differing styles.

Based on hundreds of women I've observed in the speaking industry, I've identified these common traits many women share:

- **Women have great conviction and truly want to change the world.** Whether they are business consultants/leaders, motivational speakers, athletes, artists, or scientists, they do what they do because they have a passion for it and want to inspire growth in others. In my experience, women rarely strive for commercial success as the singular end result of their work. Certainly, being successful by traditional standards (recognition, financial compensation) matters to them, and why shouldn't it? But this description of success is often treated as a by-product of women's broader goals. Women tend to look globally at how they can effect real change—and when I say *globally*, I mean it in the sense of going beyond what is immediately in front of us. Whether these goals of change are focused within their communities at a grassroots level or internationally is somewhat irrelevant. The important point is that women's motivations and convictions extend far beyond the mercenary.

- **Women see themselves as the whole of many equally vital parts.** Most women speakers who listed their profiles with my bureau put great emphasis on the volunteer roles they take on, the families they care for, and the values they personally espouse. They believe these elements are as important in describing them as people as the expertise they market professionally. More and more, women are bringing their personal lives into their presentations. *Personal has become professional.* Women recognize that authenticity resonates with their audiences and colleagues, and that real connection matters and leads to change. This whole picture matters to women in their work, as it is the entire life experience and person that informs all of the component parts.

- **Women fuel and are fueled by connections**. They are masterful at making real connections because it just comes naturally. Women generally enjoy helping others. They also step openly into a conversation, meet the whole person in front of them, and, in return, share their whole person. By *whole person*, I mean that women are unafraid to reveal who they are beyond their workday. When people are driven to help others and also reveal their own multiple layers, opportunities and synergies quickly arise. In my opinion, this is where magic takes place.

- **Women are really good at reinvention**. I cannot count the number of conversations I've had with women speakers who have achieved their vision and success through major reinvention in their lives and careers. They faced their challenges, lived through their fears, and came out on the other side with renewed vision and conviction. Women are very adept at adaptation and reinvention.

As I was thinking about these traits that I believe are predominant in women, I couldn't help thinking of one woman who boldly expresses all of them. Linda Lundstrom is a celebrated Canadian fashion designer and businesswoman who introduced the celebrated women's La Parka coat around the world, most notably throughout Canada because of its chic and luxurious "northern" feel. Linda was a maverick in adopting the lean manufacturing process in her business and is still sought-after for her expertise in that area. She gives back (in many ways) to the aboriginal communities that exist within and outside of the community in which she was raised. And she is unafraid to reveal her spiritual side, often revealing God as an important influence in her life.

Linda had to reinvent her life when her business went bankrupt (after years of great success) due to economic forces beyond her control. This was an incredibly difficult time in her life financially, professionally, and personally. Through this tragic event, Linda reinvented herself and, during that process, took the time to appreciate the world around her. She retreated to nature at her beloved cottage home with her family. I have seen Linda speak a few times and she tells her story with tremendous wit, grace, insight, and unabashed honesty. In my opinion, she is one of the best speakers I have ever heard.

Linda embraces her reinvention and steps forward boldly, saying, "Here I am, good, bad, and ugly. Let's talk!" With this, she has touched me, along with many others. I called Linda and asked her if she'd like to be listed on my roster of speakers, unsure of where she was in life. Much to my delight, she agreed.

I remember sitting at an event, listening to Linda speak. At one point in her presentation, she pointed me out and told the audience I had helped to change her life by making my phone call at that particular time. I simply couldn't believe it. First of all, I couldn't believe I had made any difference to a dynamic and successful woman like Linda! Second, by suggesting *I* had made a difference to *her*, *she* made a difference for *me* (there's that idea of women being open and honest and unafraid in an interaction—they naturally make connections and change lives).

I realized, through Linda, that we all have the power to help another person, to make a difference, and that if we feel the urge to make contact, we *should* and we *must*. We never know who will need us on their personal journey, and likewise, who we will need.

I am now in the process of my own reinvention and hope I can take Linda's lead as I move toward a new vision. I have been in the world of events and speakers for some time and I recently came to the important conclusion that I wanted to let more of my own talents shine. I have launched an online lifestyle magazine called *SlowStruck—Taking Time Is the Ultimate Rush*. This engaging online magazine shares features and contributions from many unique personalities, all focused on one central goal: encouraging small and doable changes in order to revitalize our health, our careers, and our relationships. It is an incredibly simple premise but something that we all need to remember in our fast-paced world. Our philosophy is that small changes are often what can make a monumental difference in living a meaningful life.

When I consider my own evolution and approach to my career and look at all that has led to this moment, I realize that there is that definite female stamp on it—just as in those four main characteristics I shared previously. I want to embrace a genuine quest that not only reflects my own skills, talents, and interests but also one where I feel an absolute conviction and desire to change peoples' lives for the better. It is a direction where I know that my whole person—the mom, the wife, the friend, the marketer, the creative person—will truly matter to the product. I feel like a leaf (but a brightly colored, very exuberant leaf!) on the wind, allowing myself to be completely open and excited about new connections, wherever they might arise (I know they will be in every direction). And finally, I am really comfortable with reinvention. I am fortunate to live in a culture that encourages and easily allows for reinvention . . . and I thankfully accept that gift.

The women around me have taught me, inspired me, and groomed me—most often without even knowing it. And therein lies the beauty of it all: this is just what women naturally do! I think that the greatest gift we can give to others in work and life, and to younger women in particular, is simply to be the people we naturally are. That is where we give and receive our greatest success.

Dr. Marissa Pei is an organizational psychologist, speaker, coach, and facilitator to hundreds of organizations, including Fortune 100 companies like Johnson & Johnson, Wells Fargo, AT&T, Mattel, UPS, and Bank of America.

Dr. Pei is the best-selling author of two books: *Organization Development and Consulting*, a graduate business text, and *Mommy, What Are Feelings?*, a children's book that her daughters illustrated when they were five and seven. This book, which explores the taste, touch, sight, and sound of feelings, has helped many autistic children.

She has parlayed her professional experience onto television as a "talking shrink head" on a number of ABC, Discovery, Learning Channel, and Fox specials, commenting on why people do weird things at work and other interesting human dynamics. She has also taken her experience onto the stage, as an internationally sought-after motivational speaker and lecturer in China, Europe, and throughout the United States.

She is a recipient of the 2012 Asian Entrepreneur of the Year and the 2007 Remarkable Woman of the Year Award from the National Association of Women Business Owners (NAWBO) and Asian Women Entrepreneurs (AWE). She also received the 2005 Role Model of the Year Award in Business and Media, presented by the Asian Business Association and Nordstrom.

Let's hear it for men. Let's hear it for women. Let's hear it for gender group differences.

Gender group differences have been the topic of much organizational psychology, academia, and science research. They are not stereotypes, but scientifically researched qualities that make women a little different from men.

For instance (and probably not surprising to most women), research shows that most women are more multifocus oriented than men; they are more capable of negotiating multiple ideas and projects at the same time. The flipside is that, when it comes to single-focus orientation, men are better at making decisions quickly.

Similarly, women tend to be more sensitive. We typically have more hormones, which leads to a more natural sense of compassion. It's not that men can't be sensitive or compassionate; women are just wired genetically to have a sort of natural proclivity; that is the way we are built. This can also be a negative, however. In a strategic meeting, two male participants can get into a heated argument where it feels like they are going to come to blows, but as soon as the decision is made, one guy will put his hand around the other guy's shoulder and ask, "Where are we going for lunch?" On the other hand, I have seen two women senior executives who strongly disagree on an issue and don't speak to each other for the rest of their careers.

Acknowledging and leveraging the value of gender group differences has been a long time coming. One of the areas that I consult in is strategic planning, which is traditionally a harder-science area. And when I do consulting in that area, some clients prefer that I don't bring anything too "touchy-feely" to the party. So there is some stereotyping that I am not able to see the hard side or numbers of business. That isn't true, but dealing with that assumption is one of the challenges I face. I think in finance or strategic planning, there is traditionally a stronger identification with the male perspective or orientation that gets brought to that area, and so women have to work harder for credibility there.

Early in my career, I was facilitating nine senior executives—all men—for a Fortune 50 company at its strategic retreat. We were working, as a group, on team communication. The group wanted to do some team building and some very "macho" work. I wanted very much to be respected, so after spending the day in ninety-five-degree weather and wine tasting with the group, I was trying to keep up with their drinking with limited success. Then I was handed a cigar. I didn't know the first thing about smoking cigars. So I inhaled and got sick. Normally, I wouldn't do those things, but I had to behave differently with them.

Fast forward to the present. Thankfully, women are now entrenched in business; gone are the days when I had to act like man and pretend to have balls that tucked in very well. I believe smart organizations recognize men and women each have a unique fit in the organization. We come to a place where the male natural strength comes in handy and there are times when the female natural strength comes in handy. And the best organizations are not the ones with the best people but the organizations that have the best people in the best-fit places. And I think that gender difference has a lot to do with discovering where that fit is.

I believe I live in a friendly universe and I don't have to compare myself to other people. I just stay clear and in tune with what my strengths are; I try to let go of the idea that I must do everything well and that I should always be a good fit. I try not to take things personally, to be impeccable about keeping my word, and to pay no attention to what things are said by other people. At the end of every day, I ask myself: *Have I done the best I can with the time that I have and resources I have with the ability that I have?* And if I can say *yes*, then I am a success.

Kerri Pomarolli is a popular speaker, author, and comedian. She is one of America's leading "clean" female comedians. She has been doing stand-up comedy for more than ten years and has appeared on the *Tonight Show* twenty-nine times at last count. Kerri is the author of *Guys Like Girls Named Jennie*, the humorous and moving story of one woman's search for real faith and true love, which is currently being considered for development as a film. Her new book, *Moms' Night Out and Other Things I Miss*, is being released alongside the movie *Moms' Night Out*. She has also appeared in several theatrically released movies and many documentaries, including the 2014 film *American Jesus* and 2009's *Hollywood on Fire*. She's appeared on Lifetime TV, *General Hospital*, ABC Family, and more. She lives in Los Angeles with her husband and fellow comedian, Ron McGeehee, and their two daughters.

My mother is the quintessential Christian: She never drank, she's never smoked, and she's still a virgin (joking!). She is flawless and I knew I was never going to be her. I think that has made me who I am today. We're best friends. She calls me every hour on the hour. But compared to all my Southern belle cousins, I was the black sheep of the family because I wasn't winning pageants and getting straight As and playing piano concerts. I didn't live life as a "rebel" child; I think it was just obvious I wasn't going to be put in any molds. I always felt like I was odd man out in pretty much every circle. But it made me stronger and more determined to succeed. Maybe back then it was to win everyone's approval.

I was always the type of girl who had a go-getter personality, which drew me to show business at a very young age. I had done theater seemingly my whole life and had done some television and commercials. My mother made sure that I went to college. As soon as I got my college degree, I was off to Los Angeles, where my parents dropped me off with a map and an apartment and drove back to Georgia. I cried!

I did what all kids do when they move to LA and started going on auditions. I landed small roles on *General Hospital* and *The Young and the Restless*. Interestingly, when I refused to do a nude scene in my first movie (*Deadlock*), I was cast as a blue alien instead. Go figure. At least they were flexible.

I worked three jobs, did a lot of fun things, and loved living the LA lifestyle. My entrepreneurial spirit spoke to me one day and convinced me I could start my own business. As a multitasker from an early age, I continued to audition as I started my own cellular technology business. I was running my business by day, going on auditions by night, traveling, doing television, and balancing all the plates that I could.

Faith is a really important element of my life and dictates a lot of my decisions; the most important thing in my life is my faith in God, and my life is a walking testimony. I came to the realization that a lot of the roles I was being offered were not the types of roles I wanted to take, so I figured I'd venture into comedy. My friends would probably tell you I was funny, but I never really thought of myself that way. It was a *huge* leap of faith for me.

I took a comedy class with Judy Carter. Before I went on stage, Judy looked at me and said I was really talented. A short time later, I did a stand-up routine at the Hollywood Improv. Unlike many comedians, my act was 100 percent clean—no sex, no bad language, and no bathroom humor. Soon I started meeting people in comedy. I felt these introductions were my way to cut to the front of the line, ahead of all of the other actors who were just waiting for their phones to ring.

Working in a male-dominated field, I think that funny women get a lot of props, not because of their gender but because they have to be good—you can't fake funny. There were times at the club when it was all guys and when I did a good show and earned their respect, it was a great feeling. I don't like it when female comedians get really gross and sexual on stage. They think this will make them better comedians, and that makes me really sad. I like to see women like Ellen DeGeneres, Carol Burnett, Fran Drescher, and Lucille Ball—women who don't undermine their intelligence to be funny. They're all examples of classy comedians.

There was a door guy at the Hollywood Improv who used to pray with me before shows. Little did I know then that he would end up becoming my husband, Ron McGeehee. Ron and I had the same vision: We both had faith in God and we both liked comedy. Ten years later, Ron and I have two beautiful girls and we've been able to weather the challenges of balancing our comedy careers (and the travel associated with them), family, and our faith. Without our faith, we would not have had the blessed life that we have.

That's not to say that everything has been easy. I'm on the road forty weeks out of the year, we have two kids, and I don't have a nanny! My husband is a comedian, too, and we just juggle. It's not easy, but I wouldn't trade it. Marriage is tough; in today's society, it is so much easier to get divorced than to stay married. You don't have to have the perfect marriage. Life happens. Depression happens, and if you think you are supposed to paddle that boat of marriage by yourself, that's not how life happens. Back in the old days, communities were designed to support their members, but now we don't have communities; we have Facebook. If you want an answer to something, what do you do, post it to your wall? That's not real community.

I know by the time I die, I can be proud of the things I did on this earth: raising good kids, having a great marriage to a wonderful man, and being a minister of hope and encouragement in the Lord. I have gotten to pray with women and see miracles. I have seen marriages saved. I've gotten the chance to see a woman survive Stage 4 cancer. I will be proud of the fact I had an opportunity to have one-on-one encounters with these women; perhaps I made a difference in their lives, too.

Your life is what you make of it. You can take your childhood and say that you were really bullied—oh, poor me—or you can take that experience and say that you know how to laugh now and get yourself out of a really bad situation. I was picked on as a child and I think that helped shape who I am. I'm pretty tough now; fortunately or unfortunately, I know how to handle myself in really brutal situations. I know how to handle a drunk heckler in a club. I know how to negotiate tough business deals. Once I was on my way home with this scary cab driver. He started hitting on me in a weird neighborhood. I just told him my Italian dad was in the Mafia and I was in witness protection and he stopped hitting on me. I've used humor as a coping mechanism on many occasions.

When I was asked to do comedy at my high-school reunion, I thought about the girls who had been mean to me when I was in high school. Although painful, with the passing of time and age, I realized that "hurting people are hurting people." They are hurt somewhere within their souls and they lash out. I had never been so nervous before going up to perform. So when the audience started to fall out laughing, it was one of those God-given moments where everything was perfect for thirty minutes, on stage with my funny, cute husband. I felt like it was redemption of sorts—coming back home and feeling really great about it. Plus, I fit into my skinny pants!

So, women, pat yourselves on the back and know that you are having an impact on the world by what you're doing in your lives, whatever that happens to be. There is nothing you shouldn't try if you have the desire. Be willing to make a "left turn" in your life for a new opportunity. I think when you take a leap of faith, it always pays off. Even if you fail, you were willing to take the jump and you'll land wherever you are supposed to be.

Kathy Quintana brings more than thirty-five years of experience, including an extensive background in operations and finance, to HUB International Insurance Services, Inc., which specializes in commercial, health, and personal insurance. Kathy currently manages the Los Angeles and Newport Beach offices for HUB and is responsible for all aspects of these operations. She serves on the executive committee for both the Los Angeles and Newport Beach offices.

Kathy has been with HUB International for fifteen years, where she has held various management, operational, and financial roles. In her existing role, she directly has management oversight for both the Employee Benefits and Personal Lines operations in Los Angeles.

Prior to working at HUB, Kathy served for twenty-four years at Sedgwick Insurance Brokers, which subsequently was acquired by Marsh & McLennan Companies. In her role at Sedgwick, Kathy was executive vice president and ran the Irvine and Orange, California, offices for the firm. There she specialized in operations and finance and directly managed the claims management services department for all national self-funded and high-deductible workers' compensation programs.

Kathy is a native of Southern California and attended UCLA. She spends her free time as a founding member of the Global Women Foundation, the umbrella organization for the California Women's Conference. Kathy's management experience allows her to mentor, guide, and support young women coming into the business world by providing them with the tools they need to grow and develop in their careers.

Kathy lives in Huntington Beach, California, and is a member of Seacliff Country Club, where she enjoys supporting her local community.

There are always challenges and opportunities in everything we do in life, including our careers. Being a woman in a male-dominated industry gave me the challenge of breaking into the "boys' club" that has dominated business and institutions for centuries. Women operate very differently than men, and that can be considered both a detriment and a benefit. It's a challenge to break the old mold that so many are used to operating in. For those who dislike change, breaking through to a new way of doing things is uncomfortable and therefore not well received. A benefit of being a woman is that I can look at and evaluate things differently. It's not that my way of seeing the world is right or wrong, but rather that there is value in a new and different perspective. Female intuition, when used appropriately, is the best asset a woman can bring to the table. It has served me well.

So has being myself. In a male-dominated industry, trying to behave like a man does not work—at least it wouldn't have worked for me. It doesn't come off as real unless that's who you really are. Imagine a man coming into a female-dominated business and trying to act like a woman. What's the point? The beauty of diversity in the workplace is that each gender brings something important to the table to round out the decision making.

I do believe my success is due in large part to the fact that I evaluate and handle things differently than my male counterparts. I do not come from the sales background that my male colleagues typically rose through. I come from a grassroots background and worked my way up from the bottom. I have sat in every seat on the bus. I can put myself in the other person's shoes, whether he or she sits at the reception desk, at the service desk, in the accounting department, wherever. That has enabled me to advocate for those people who depend on me for their own career growth. I understand what they do and what they struggle with, and I can mentor them and help them understand the steps they must take in order to excel in their careers and achieve their goals.

In some ways, of course, being a woman has felt like a detriment most of my career. I just haven't allowed it to get the best of me. That would have been the easier route many times. It's easy to give up when you think you can't make a difference or when you aren't being allowed the same opportunities as men. So you need certain attributes: belief in yourself, validated by those who support you; persistence, so that if things don't work one way you'll figure out another; and a few good women and men who believe in you and mentor you along the way.

Most important, there's no substitute for hard work. If you are serious about climbing high on the corporate ladder, then your time is not your own. It requires doing whatever it takes to get the job done. It requires coming in early and staying late. It requires earning someone's appreciation by making her or his job a little easier. All of these things get noticed by those senior people who can make or break you. It's your job not only to make your clients happy but to make your bosses look good. If you can do that and still keep your identity and power intact, then you're going to be successful. The people who matter to your career will help you move forward. At least that has been my experience in getting to where I am today.

I am honored to have had the opportunity to be one of the female pioneers in my industry. This is still a business in which the majority of senior managers are men. I have cracked the glass ceiling but was never given the opportunity to break completely through it. The next generations of female executives will have that opportunity, provided those of us who came before them do not fail to guide, train, and enlighten them.

We have an obligation and a responsibility to mentor and guide those women who come after us. Men have learned the secret formula because they have had decades, even centuries, to figure it out. They support each other—the old boys' club continues to thrive, decade after decade. They have learned how to nurture and promote each other. Women must learn to do the same thing. We need to teach younger women that it's about respect and teamwork, not cattiness and jealousy. I don't mean that all women are catty and jealous. I mean that healthy competition is good, and men have learned well how to play in that arena. Women are still learning the ropes, and it's up to those of us who have succeeded in that arena to help the younger ones figure it out.

And we can do that well. Women bring a "sisterhood" of understanding that men cannot. We can talk about things and just understand each other and where we're coming from. We bring a sensitivity to employee issues that, I believe, goes a little deeper than a man's ability to understand. Maybe it's that nurturing instinct. Although I have never been a mother, I know that I nurture others without mothering them. I'm not sure you find that skill in many men.

Which women nurtured, influenced, and inspired me? The first one is going to sound hokey, but it's true. When I was a teenager, Mary Tyler Moore had a show in which she worked in the big city of Minneapolis. That show fascinated me, and from that point forward, I knew I wanted to be in the corporate world and experience the big city. I won't say the character Mary Tyler Moore played influenced me, but the concept of a woman working in a corporate environment did.

Once I got into the corporate world, there was only one woman who deeply influenced me. I was in my twenties when I met her, and I was already a supervisor. I was captivated by this woman's polish and grace, combined with her ability to do the tough stuff. I knew that skill set was what I wanted to emulate. I can look back now and say I believe I accomplished that.

When I first began to supervise others, I had a female boss who took me under her wing and taught me a lot about the technical side of the business. She was strong and very intelligent. I was and am extremely grateful to her. She believed in me enough to stand up for me in this very male-dominated industry. She was the pioneer woman who saw the skills and abilities in me that I hadn't yet seen in myself. She touched me deeply, because she took the time to believe in me until I grew and strengthened my own belief in myself. Because of her, I had the confidence and skill to replace her when she left the firm. That was my first management job. Even more important, she gave me the conviction that it is my responsibility to pay it forward to other women who follow after me.

Paying it forward consists mostly of helping women grow and advance in my industry, but there are some general principles I'd suggest to any young woman in business.

Above all, be yourself. You are a beautiful being with a lot of inner strength—none of us truly realizes how much lies within ourselves until we have to tap into it. Do not try to be something or someone you are not. Everybody sees a phony for who she is. And always remember that there's nothing more beautiful than a woman who shows vulnerability and strength in one package. That's something only a woman can do. Embrace it and use it to your advantage.

Kimberly S. Reed is the founder and CEO of Reed Development Group. Her company provides innovative, custom solutions in the areas of diversity and inclusion strategy, leadership, and business and personal development for corporations, institutions, and individuals, including several professional athletes. Kimberly lectures at the Wharton School of Business, Villanova University, Temple University, Howard University, and Sharon Baptist Bible Institute. She is a dynamic speaker and trains clients in public speaking as well.

Prior to starting her own company, Kimberly served as a diversity and inclusion strategist for PricewaterhouseCoopers, Campbell Soup Company, Merrill Lynch, and Deloitte. She is also a senior partner at Ascendant Strategy, a branding, management, and literary strategy company specializing in increasing visibility for executive clientele. In addition, she mentors more than sixty college students of color who aspire to be in business and entrepreneurship.

There weren't always seats at the corporate table for women, especially women of color, so I was very privileged to have a career in the corporate world for more than thirteen years. I was especially blessed to be in positions where I could ensure that other women, students, and emerging leaders of color also had these opportunities and exposure at the corporate table. Now, as an entrepreneur, being a woman is a huge advantage, more so than in corporate America, because woman-led businesses are thriving and growing around our country. I don't take my role lightly at all because I know my path was paved by many women in corporations and many business owners before me.

As an African American woman and as a diversity practitioner, I am excited that companies are embracing diversity and inclusion and infusing this into their cultures as business objectives. Not only is it a good thing, but it really puts me at an advantage as an individual. It's created a lot of opportunities for me with global and nonprofit organizations, as well as in universities as a teacher.

Being able to see new opportunities through three different lenses—as a corporate executive, an African American, and a woman—has been of great benefit to me as an entrepreneur. In fact, the greatest challenges I've had were not as an entrepreneur but in my corporate career. I rose quickly on the corporate ladder, and the higher I climbed, the more my age became an issue as it related to those to whom I reported. At some point I think the color of my skin limited my opportunities as well.

I will say that being a woman has never been a disadvantage in working with men. I love working for men. They have fewer insecurities, and they will give you exposure and let you shine, if you will. I'm sad to say that it has been women who have been a challenge to work with in both corporate and entrepreneurial settings. Men open up their Rolodexes to me with no trepidation. Here's the key, though: I think it's how you play the game. For me, when you have a strong sense of self and "sexy" in your mind, it is very easy to navigate and work with men. Women who are insecure and who don't have that "mental sexiness" have a very hard time with men.

Of course, many women have different experiences from mine. I coach women lawyers, and they have huge challenges in the workplace with men and the competition for work, client exposure, in the partner ranks, and with their peers. As I climbed the corporate ladder, there were men who had my back, but in other kinds of businesses that still isn't the case. And unfortunately, many women don't seek out men as mentors to help them fight the good fight.

That is one area, though, where being a woman gives me a special advantage over men: coaching executive women. Men don't see women through the same lens as other women do. They don't have the same sets of challenges and triumphs. Men cannot really coach women to understand how to play the game at the top because they play the game under an extremely different set of rules. I can coach executive women as a person who has felt and experienced the same challenges, woes, and triumphs that they have.

I owe my personal success to a lot of people but particularly to the examples set by my mother, grandmothers, and grandfather. They taught me always to pay it forward and pass on to others the blessings that you received. Also, they taught me to be a person of integrity and to keep my word, and they instilled a strong work ethic in me. My mom was a corporate woman. She set some great examples for me in addition to the ones I just listed. She showed me that the image you show the corporate world isn't merely external but something that comes from inside. It's being who you are and not changing your identity. She taught me to develop myself as a person and to seek out opportunities to provide excellence to an organization. My desire to do my very best for my clients came from my grandparents, who instilled that in their children and grandchildren. I attribute everything to the foundation and the important characteristics my parents and grandparents gave me.

I'll mention three other people who have been great influences in my life:

Charisse Lillie is president of the Comcast Foundation. She is ultra-successful, a woman I'd describe as a "quiet storm." She was an attorney at a top firm in Philadelphia and was a senior human resources executive. She now contributes her efforts to many community organizations. She really knows how to play the game at the top in a great way. She is a mentor of mine who reinforced what my mother and others have shown me throughout the years: never change your individuality, keep your integrity, do your best, and you will get recognized. You don't have to step over other women or cut down other women. You don't have to play those negative games to be successful.

Dr. Westina Matthews Shatteen was one of the top people on Wall Street. She taught me the same thing: It is important as a black woman that you don't change who you are to become successful. You have to be three times better than your counterparts, and, unfortunately, that is how it has always been. But it is up to you to decide how you want to be in your skin. No matter how tough a business you are in, you must always persevere and outrun people who are not true to themselves and to the objectives at hand.

Rosemary Tuner is a president of one of the largest UPS districts in the United States and one of the few African American women to hold that position. She taught me some great lessons. Accentuate the positive and develop the skills that you desire. Make sure that people see your talent. Go where the action is, get outside your comfort zone, and connect with great people—people who are better and stronger than you are now.

Not everyone who affects you deeply does so in a positive way, but we need to learn and grow from all our experiences. I was at a professional services firm where I reported to a woman who was extremely insecure. She surrounded herself with "yes women" to whom she obviously felt superior. I was one of two African American women on her staff. One time I made a presentation that received great reviews across the board. The next day this woman called me in, and I could tell she wasn't happy with me. She said, "Kim, you always give me 'Cadillac' when all I request of you is 'Pinto.'" These are two types of cars that are typically driven by black people. I paused in amazement that she said something like that. Then I said to her, "I'm sorry that you were not happy with the presentation and that you felt I gave a little bit more than you thought I should have, but I think a better analogy would be a BMW or a Mercedes. I can probably relate to those cars a little bit better." I didn't want to come out of my skin by stooping to that level of ignorance. But I felt much of her response was because of the color of my skin and what she thought I should be versus who I am.

Some advice I'd give to women starting their own companies: First, you've got to get your "board of directors." By that, I mean your mentors, your sponsors, and other people who have been successful and have blazed the trail for you. Your network equals your net worth. You can't be afraid to take healthy risks in business or in life. You have to learn to love who you are in the skin that you are in. Sometimes we get knocked down, but we can't stay down. Get back up and try it again. You have to weather the storm without a shadow of a doubt that there is a rainbow to come.

Janet C. Salazar is the CEO and founder of IMPACT Leadership 21, a movement and a platform committed to accelerating and transforming women's global leadership at the highest level of influence in the twenty-first century. She is also the president and cofounder of Maverick Vision International Advisors, a New York–based global firm providing highly specialized consulting, coaching, training, and advisory services on multicultural leadership development, strategies, and business platforms.

Janet also serves as the permanent representative to the United Nations at Foundation for the Support of the United Nations (FSUN), an international NGO in General Consultative Status with the United Nations Economic and Social Council (ECOSOC) and associated with the United Nations Department of Public Information (UN DPI). In addition, she serves as board treasurer and public relations director of the executive committee of NGOs associated with UN DPI, tasked to represent more than 1,400 global NGOs to the United Nations.

She is a certified executive coach and a confidential advisor to top senior and emerging women executives and leaders, CEOs, expatriates, nonprofit leaders, diplomats, entrepreneurs, artists, and visionaries around the world.

Janet serves on the international steering committee of the Asian Women's Leadership University Project, whose goal is to establish a world-class liberal arts university for women in Asia based on the "seven sisters" model in the United States. She also serves on the boards of several non-profit organizations.

Janet holds a bachelor's degree in hotel and restaurant management from the University of Baguio, Philippines, graduating with honors. She also attended Saint Louis University–Philippines, where she studied mass communications.

There are certainly challenges for women who want to rise to leadership in a society where businesses and institutions are traditionally led by men. But personally I haven't encountered major challenges related to my sex because I have always been able to enlist male advocates on my side. At the United Nations, in my business, and in my community activities, I have always found a way to collaborate with men.

Of course, there are differences in the way men and women approach things. For example, I'm thinking of something I noticed working with the executive committee of nongovernmental organizations (NGOs) to the United Nations, where I serve as a board member and treasurer. Last year we had about four men, including our chair. I noticed some interesting differences in decision making. The women tended to overanalyze and wanted to know the details in everything before we acted on a resolution. The men would read something once or twice and make a decision. That is a very common phenomenon, and I think that's innate with most women, including me.

There are many other behavior patterns, such as patience and tenacity, that are unique to women. We don't give up. We are very resilient in bouncing back from failure and disappointment. This has helped me a lot in terms of my success. Flexibility is very important, too. We are able to multitask, something I do well. It is scientifically proven that men are not as good at multitasking as women. With my own staff, I am very sensitive to assigning particular projects or presenting opportunities. I use my knowledge of what a person is good at and what his or her natural talents are. For example, I will not assign my male team member a task I know will require a lot of multitasking. I want to set people up for success and leverage their talents.

I'm fortunate to have had many great women in my life as influences. The first and most fundamental is my mom. She was widowed when I was five. She was only twenty-two, but she never remarried. She grew a business and a restaurant, and she taught my brother and

178

me how to run it while we were growing up. My mom is very tenacious and hardworking and very selfless. She never worried about herself. She worried about me and my brother, about providing for us. I attribute everything I have accomplished to her.

The most important woman in my professional life is Judy Lerner. Judy has been a leading peace activist since the 1950s and is still active as a representative from Peace Action International to the United Nations. I used to visit her every other week in her apartment, and she would give me great advice about women and success. Judy is now in her nineties. When we launched IMPACT Leadership 21, a movement and a platform committed to transforming women's global leadership at the highest level of influence in the twenty-first century, on 12/12/12, she was there to speak, and she was fabulous!

Another woman I want to mention is my friend Michaela Walsh. Michaela is the founder of Women's World Banking, a pioneer in global microfinancing, giving low-income women the finance, savings, and insurance services they need to start small businesses. She was selfless in sharing her experience and wisdom with me as I was starting IMPACT Leadership 21. I still call her when I need advice.

Women need to help each other this way. It is a sad reality that many women who have the capacity, resources, and opportunity aren't getting together with women who are just starting or building their careers or starting their own businesses. Women in positions of influence need to be mentoring and sponsoring others. So I look for opportunities to open doors for women. I devote time to mentoring the younger generation. I take on clients who have high potential but are young and need the insight of older, accomplished women on how to be successful.

Paying it forward should be one of the top missions of any woman who has been successful in her career. So I'll do a little of that now with a few words of advice that I really believe in:

Never stop seeking opportunities. There are many opportunities out there for us to succeed, but they don't just come to you.

Collaborate. Learn how to reach out and build a high-quality network. Do not go about building your network based on what you are going to get out of this or that person. Instead, focus on how you can help that person, even if she or he is already very successful. People can tell whether you have a genuine desire to connect with them or whether you just want something from them.

Never give up. If there is one trait that all successful people share, it is tenacity. Don't take too many things personally. A lot of women in the workplace get too emotional because they are taking things too personally. Don't do that. Just move on, work hard, and do your best.

Lucy Sanders is CEO and co-founder of the National Center for Women & Information Technology (NCWIT) and also serves as executive-in-residence for the ATLAS Institute at the University of Colorado at Boulder.

Lucy has worked in R&D and executive positions at AT&T Bell Labs, Lucent Bell Labs, and Avaya Labs. In 1996, she was awarded the Bell Labs Fellow Award, the highest technical accomplishment bestowed at the company, and she has six patents in communications technology.

Lucy serves on several high-tech start-up and non-profit boards and frequently advises young technology companies. She has served on advisory boards and commissions for the University of California–Berkeley, the National Academies, and the US Department of Commerce. She has received several prestigious awards.

Lucy received her BS and MS degrees in computer science from Louisiana State University and the University of Colorado at Boulder, respectively.

As a woman in computing, I am acutely aware of women's underrepresentation in the field. That is a sad thing, but it also represents a tremendous opportunity. What would women invent if they were inventing the technology of the future, the technology upon which our world increasingly depends? We don't know, alas, because most technology today is created or invented by men. But I know that when women are designing technical products and services alongside men, they will not only solve problems differently but also solve different problems.

Members of underrepresented groups in any discipline or sector face significant cultural challenges. Bias is often unintended, but it is bias nonetheless, and it creates institutional barriers to success in hiring and promotion. Understanding the social science research on underrepresentation can make a tremendous difference for technical leaders and for the underrepresented themselves. Those underrepresented also can feel isolated and outnumbered, causing them to feel like they don't belong or can't contribute.

That said, I'm not sure that as a woman in my field I really behave in a different way than the men. I may have had to work harder in some cases to overcome the fact that women are not normally present in the kind of technology leadership positions I have held. I was fortunate to have worked for Bell Labs, an organization with diversity and inclusion in their corporate DNA. That made it far easier for me, I think, than for others that I know. I didn't really have much time to think about it. I was creating great technology, raising a family, having fun. At times, organizational barriers annoyed me, especially if I thought they were slowing me down.

I've been successful partly because I listen carefully to feedback, incorporate what's good about it, and forge ahead. I am an inventor. I like to take up unformed ideas, help shape them, iterate on them, and then go around again until finally something of value emerges. I am a big-picture thinker who also loves to dig into details. I am collaborative and transparent.

Designing technology is a creative process, one in which we bring the collection of our life experiences to the table—our hopes, dreams, passions. Technology enables the human race to mitigate some of the major challenges of our day. It's important that the female point of view is part of this critical and creative process. For example, women need to be helping create health services software and social networking platforms, but they also need to be involved in the implementation of security software and vital communications systems.

There have always been women in this field—not many, but some have been prominent: Ada Lovelace, Grace Hopper, Jean Sammet, and other women helped invent the computer and computer programming languages.

On a personal level, my high school math teacher Sandra McCalla taught me how to program an early desktop computer and encouraged me to persist in technology. She went above and beyond to make sure we were well versed in the emerging computing space. I try to pass that on in my own career. I lead a nonprofit, the National Center for Women & Information Technology (NCWIT). We work in every state to ensure that young women have access to education and careers in computing. We welcome involvement by both women and men in our programs.

On a more personal level, it's hard to give advice in a book like this one because advice is so dependent on an individual's context. What works for me may not work for others. But I think it's important in any context to stay open to life's detours and see what opportunities may lie down those roads. Some of my most successful moments were unplanned and quite unexpected. The important thing was that I noticed the opportunity and capitalized on it.

Kristen Sharma has made a significant difference by inspiring and healing many lives through her companies, college, teachings, singing, and songwriting. She has traveled to more than thirty-five countries as an advocate for body, mind, and spirit education. She was honored as Female Entrepreneur of the Year in 2010 by the governor of Iowa as the woman who made the most significant difference for others in the state.

As an entrepreneur for more than twenty-five years, Kristen has owned eight successful businesses. She founded and directs the East-West School of Integrative Healing Arts and Massage Therapy College, an award-winning school in her native Iowa. She also founded and directs A Massage Oasis, a holistic healing and therapeutic massage program for hospitals, corporations, and university campuses.

In addition to being a serial entrepreneur, she is a wife, mother, singer, songwriter, artist, published author, and international speaker. Kristen is also a Platinum Partner graduate of the Anthony Robbins University Leadership Academy and served as an advisor and consultant to the Deepak Chopra Center for Living in San Diego, California.

Kristen is online at www.kristensharma.com.

For most of my life, I really didn't understand gender-specific roles. As a child, there were no "girl" chores or "boy" chores in my family; there were just chores that needed to be done. Along with my brother and sister, my parents taught us to work hard, use our gifts, and make a difference. We were encouraged to be leaders, ask questions, and always, always continue to learn. My mission is to inspire myself and others to heal and enlighten the world using our God-given gifts. I have had several businesses over the last twenty-five years, all of which helped or inspired people. I am also a singer and a songwriter and I carry my mission with me in all the work I do.

In 2006, I was hired as a consultant for the design and launch of the Deepak Chopra Center for Living in San Diego, which is a holistic healing and education center. While working on the concept and curriculum for the Center, I felt a natural love for the idea of helping people through healing. On my return to the Midwest, I created my own holistic healing projects in the form of a healing arts college and a corporate massage therapy spa program, A Massage Oasis. I love massage! Many years ago, after fracturing my vertebrae in high school, doctors predicted that I could be in a wheelchair by the age of forty. It was massage that made the difference and now enables me to live an active and busy life that I love.

Now it gives me great satisfaction to see that more than 200 students have a new career through graduating from the East-West School and many continue to work in the field. A Massage Oasis continues to grow and help organizations look after the wellness of their employees and improving morale, attendance, and overall health. The service is extremely popular at all locations, which lets me know that we are making a difference.

I also organize a health and wellness conference called "Be Your Best" and about 95 percent of the attendees are women. It is not intended as a "women's event," but I think women have an interest in wanting to be the best they can be, pass it on, and shine the light on others. Many of our staff, students, and clients are women. I've learned that women really do create cultures where we work together as a team with compassion, caring, and kindness—"leadership with kindness" is how I like to think of it. Although I've found that men are wonderful problem solvers, women tend to want to help people feel great, feel nurtured, and show compassion. Women tend to be natural healers and therapists.

Currently, I am excited to be writing and recording custom songs of inspiration for celebrities and high-profile clients. I am also leading the creation of the theme song for the Global Women Foundation and California Women's Conference that we hope will reach millions to empower women, raise awareness of the poor conditions for many women across the world, and inspire women and men everywhere to work together to heal the world. The theme for the conference and the song is "Together, we are better."

We are better together! We need each other—men need women, and women need men. We all have our struggles. People, for the most part, do the best they can for each other with what they have. There's no better feeling for me than to watch my colleagues, students, staff, faculty, and clients work together, go the extra mile, exceed expectations, make a significant difference for others, and do it with heart for the betterment of the human race.

Janet Switzer is unique among business experts as the woman who has created and executed highly successful day-to-day income-generation strategies for many of the world's top celebrity entrepreneurs. She's a number-one bestselling author (*Instant Income: Strategies That Bring in the Cash for Small Businesses, Innovative Employees and Occasional Entrepreneurs*), as well as the coauthor of *The Success Principles: How to Get From Where You Are to Where You Want to Be*, a *New York Times* and *USA Today* bestseller that has been published in twenty-seven languages.

Her popular column featuring topics of interest to small-business owners is syndicated to more than 220 media outlets worldwide. She has also counseled thousands of companies and entrepreneurs in the areas of generating immediate revenue and securing long-term success.

Not that long ago, when it came to pursuing their careers, women were forced into an "either/or" situation. In order to be successful in her career, the perception was that a woman had to either put everything into her job or be faced with choosing personal goals (such as raising a family or caring for elderly parents) to the forfeiture of career opportunities she deserved.

Fortunately, technology has leveled the playing field for women today, who can now make tangible contributions to any and all fields—but most importantly in the area of entrepreneurship. Today, women start businesses at a rate of two-to-one over men; more than two-thirds of all new businesses worldwide are started by women. Women-owned businesses are also uniquely recognized by the US government, which offers a variety of incentives to encourage entrepreneurship. Not to be left out, corporations now encourage women's entrepreneurship through monetary support of special initiatives.

Perhaps most important, however, is that it's no longer a tough choice between raising a family and owning a business. Internet-based businesses, virtual offices, flextime employment, and job sharing are but a few ways in which women have taken back control over their professional and personal lives.

Many women have also emerged as experts in the small-business category. For decades, we saw our male counterparts reign as the top-selling business authors, most popular business speakers, and most talked-about business advisors. This is ironic since women are more likely to pursue continuing education to ensure they are well versed in innovations that can improve efficiency and ROI; they purchase some 85 percent of business-related books and a significant percentage of other learning tools.

As a woman business author, I'm often asked how I conduct business differently than my male colleagues. While I generally don't speak in generalities, I will in this instance. **Women are inherently**

more detail oriented (I certainly fall into this category), while men, at least in the small-business category, more often take the role of big-picture thinkers or visionaries.

When it comes to teaching a marketing strategy or revenue-generation system or making a sale, I'm constantly attentive to ensuring that entrepreneurs understand every step of the process or have every bit of information they need to make a buying decision. When I teach entrepreneurs, I'm focused not just on the what-to-do, but on the step-by-step "how-to-do." I like to overdeliver by providing lots of detail. I believe this eye for detail—a trait commonly attributed to women—has contributed significantly to my success. Very little at my company is left to chance—which is quite deliberate, and which has served me well during my career.

Today, my reputation has been built on the care I take in explaining the process in the books I write, and in my speeches, newsletters, and home-study courses.

Behind this ability to "explain in detail" is two decades of work—not as a visionary, but as the day-to-day income-generation strategist for a wide variety of small companies.

For the first twenty years of my career, I was the woman in the background behind many of the world's top celebrity entrepreneurs, authors, and speakers, as well as countless brick-and-mortar businesses. During that time, I had the opportunity to hone my capabilities in developing revenue streams for small businesses. In some cases, I didn't get paid unless I brought in the cash, so as you can imagine, I got really good at refining strategies that delivered reliable cash flow. When I wrote my book, *Instant Income*, I compiled those strategies that are quick to execute and that bring in the cash quickly—strategies that I had honed and refined over nearly twenty years.

As a woman entrepreneur who works often with other women entrepreneurs, I've seen some unique qualities that help women excel in their field.

Women tend to be great communicators and even better relationship builders. This really becomes valuable in small business when creating strategic alliances, introducing people to your big vision, and nurturing relationships that will pay off over time. It's exceptionally helpful to have a relationship-building attitude when it comes to customers. For example, my company focuses on delivering useful and well-thought-out products to our many long-time readers and subscribers. And though I may not be the one creating the biggest stir at a multispeaker event or the one attracting hundreds of thousands of opt-ins from a single e-mail, my readers are established business owners and loyal followers who convert really well into buyers of our products and services. As an author, I know I would rather have 100,000 loyal readers who respond to virtually any offer I broadcast than a million Web site visitors who don't buy because I'm focused on numbers instead of relationships.

Women are good at taking a big project, breaking it down into parts, and seeing well in advance what's needed to complete it successfully. Smart businesswomen tend to be planners. While they can visualize the big goals they want, they also have the ability to see the necessary steps required to bring those goals to fruition. In my book with Jack Canfield, *The Success Principles*, we wrote a chapter called "Chunk It Down"—the idea that any big goal can be achieved (and seem less daunting) by breaking it down into manageable tasks. Women are good at doing that. Not only does this skill keep you focused on the end game, but it keeps you from spending time and energy on tasks that don't matter to the ultimate outcome. I think women sometimes have a sense that they need to work harder than men to be successful as business owners. This isn't true, of course, but the perception is still there. Chunking it down is a strategy that will keep women working *smarter,* not harder—and help them be exponentially more successful as a result.

Women in business naturally tend to "pay it forward" to other women just starting out. I am always happy to see women's entrepreneurial networks in action—where more established women business owners advise, mentor, and act as a sounding board for younger women or women just beginning their careers. In fact, it's a perfect example of a well-known success principle at work: "Success leaves clues." For anything that you want to accomplish, there's likely someone else who has already achieved that goal—especially in the field of entrepreneurship. Seeking out these established experts, asking questions, and acting on their advice is often the key to achieving goals faster. Not only are women natural seekers of information, but they're also good recipients of advice and energetic followers and implementers of any strategies that are given to them.

Rose Tafoya is a highly motivated entrepreneur, author, and speaker. In her journey, she has over thirty years' experience in all aspects of new business development, sales, event and project coordination, marketing, executive team building management, communication, and networking. Her extensive experience includes fund-raising and event programming for nonprofit and for-profit organizations. She has created, programmed, and implemented many fundraising, trade show, community, and career expo events. She contributes her expertise, support, and energy to the California Women's Conference as director of programming, and contributes to WomenNetwork.com and the *Huffington Post*. Rose's marketing and communication education has led her toward transformational workshop facilitation, public speaking, product building, and novel writing. Her passion for motivating youth prompted the development and production of Tigercamp—a character education youth camp and, most recently, RoseTafoya.com, a transformational service company specializing in helping youth and adults achieve success by providing iGlowSpirit travel adventures locally and abroad, Passion Test and Purpose Workshops, and CAbi® career opportunities for women. All these services and products promote confidence, clarity, brilliance, and living life with passion and purpose.

I think that men and women are equal in our ability and opportunity to strive toward our aspirations and excel at all levels. The only difference I see is that women might have a stronger desire to nurture and comfort, that they are more sensitive to the needs of others. That's not to say that men can't be that way, but our society has conditioned women to be the patient nurturers and to act that way in the home, workplace, and community.

I think the compassion that women have draws me into supporting, motivating, and inspiring others—into being a role model for women, men, and children.

There are benefits and drawbacks to women's compassionate nature. Sometimes women get so caught up in the role of caregiver, get their compassion levels turned up so high, that it holds things up. They lose their impetus in driving a project forward.

But in the long run, when you are connected with people at all levels, you get better results. In my business, it has helped tremendously to get in touch with what's going on in my employees' daily and personal lives and validate who they are as people. It has helped me to retain employees and keep them happy. Forging those personal connections, patience, and the ability to step back and see the big picture have been important to my own success. So have three other qualities I value highly: perseverance, tenacity, and curiosity. I never give up. And I have always been curious. I have a genuine desire to know and understand the world and the people around me. I feel successful when I am connecting with others and inspiring minds, personal awareness, and people's passion for life.

In fact, helping people discover their true passion in life is probably the most important and rewarding thing I do. When you begin to do what you truly love, what you are passionate about, your life opens up. Don't worry about how you're going to do it. Becoming truly clear about *what* you love in your life will lead you to the *how*. *What* do you love? *What* are you on this planet to do? When you know what that is and open yourself to it, then *how* to do it will come easily. Being open to possibilities and throwing away your fear and false beliefs will give you the power to make that personal journey and enjoy the trip.

There have been two women in my life who have been especially helpful in inspiring my curiosity and my passion for pursuing new possibilities. The first was an elementary-school teacher who instilled in me a passion for reading and my desire to learn about the diversity in our world. She was a show-and-tell kind of teacher who taught me how powerful words and stories can affect our hearts, minds, and souls. I owe to her much of my positive approach to life.

The mystery novelist Elizabeth George has also had a profound effect on my life. I used to attend the Maui Writers Conference, and one year all the nonfiction workshops I wanted to attend were full. This led me to Ms. George's fiction workshop. She was a tough and demanding teacher. At the end of the week, though, she suggested that I ought to consider writing fiction. That led me to write my first novel, *I of a Tiger*. I spent the next year writing the book, giving it so much of my time and attention that it became a challenge to my marriage, which ended in divorce. And yet, writing that book led me to my true spirit and purpose. The creative process got me out of the cage I was in. That year was a major turning point in my life, and it taught me how important it is to share my story and follow my passion. I haven't looked back.

JJ Virgin, the author of the *New York Times* bestseller *The Virgin Diet: Drop 7 Foods, Lose 7 Pounds, Just 7 Days,* is one of America's foremost fitness and nutrition experts, a popular media personality, and a public speaker. With more than twenty-five years in the health and fitness industry, she most recently has been involved in holistic nutrition and functional medicine.

The Virgin Diet has been on the bestseller lists in the *Wall Street Journal, USA Today,* the *Chicago Tribune,* and numerous other media outlets. JJ is also the author of *Six Weeks to Sleeveless and Sexy,* published by Simon & Schuster Gallery, and she costarred on the TLC reality series *Freaky Eaters.*

JJ is recognized in the weight-loss industry as an expert, and has turned the most challenging weight-loss-resistant cases into unqualified successes. She offers a sensible, no-fail approach to nutrition and fitness. She has worked with high-performance athletes, CEOs, and celebrities and, for two years, appeared as the nutrition expert on the *Dr. Phil Show.*

She is a certified nutrition specialist, a certified health and fitness instructor with advanced certifications in nutrition, personal training, and aging, and is board-certified in holistic nutrition.

To borrow from Charles Dickens, it was the best of times, it was the worst of times. My soon-to-be *New York Times* bestselling book, *The Virgin Diet,* was on the cusp of being published. It was an exciting, whirlwind time and I had invested an incredible amount of time and a massive amount of money to make it to this point.

But the whirlwind stopped quickly when I learned my teen-age son, Grant, had been severely injured in a near-fatal accident. I couldn't just put my book on hold; I was the family breadwinner, and I was heavily financially invested in it. More important, though, I needed to be with my son. I moved from my home in Palm Desert two hours away to be closer to the hospital in Los Angeles, so that I could be with him twelve to fifteen hours a day.

Overwhelmed, frightened, and panicked, I did the only thing I knew to do: I called in the troops.

I sent out a 911 to all of my friends—both business and personal. They literally showed up in droves, helping me in every aspect of my life. I had my business friends who aided in dealing with matters concerning the book, while my personal friends helped me keep my life in some semblance of order. Interestingly, although about half of my group of friends are men, 90 percent of those who showed up over the next four months to help were women.

My story has a happy ending. My son recovered from his injuries and I successfully launched my book. But the experience confirmed something that I had always believed: that women, by nature, are naturally more collaborative than competitive, and more collaborative in general than men.

Collaboration is the cornerstone of my business. A large percentage of my marketing is accomplished by collaborating with other health-care professionals. After all, we generally don't buy one book on a favorite subject; we collect books. So when my peers recommend my books to their patients and clients, it is incredibly powerful.

I also develop my books and programs through team collaboration. Usually, the collaboration process works quite well. Sometimes collaboration can turn into a bit too much of a democracy, with a lot of talk back and forth and not enough action! In those circumstances, I like to explain what we're going to do and why so that we can move forward constructively with no bruised feelings.

When it comes to collaboration, respect and trust are critical. Without these elements, the integrity of this collaborative effort can come into question. I have a group of about thirty peers I collaborate with regularly and we all organically understand the boundaries— we look to serve each other before we ever ask for support and we ensure that whatever we are collaborating on is mutually beneficial to both brands.

One wonderful example of collaboration is mentorship. I have had some incredible mentors along the way, and the ones who have really helped me make the biggest leaps the fastest focused on mindset more than strategies and fundamentals. One mentor in particular repeatedly told me that the only limitations I had were the limitations in my mind; that phrase is my mantra when I am pushing myself to a higher level and fear shows up.

Beyond being a mentor for other women, one of the biggest ways we can support and collaborate with other women, especially those starting out, is to share our struggles with them so they understand what is normal. So often, all people see is success; they don't see the dark hours. So when a little challenge pops up, they quit. We need to share the struggle as well as the success so they know that this is all part of the journey. Ultimately, by reaching out for help when my son was in the hospital, my book launch was far more successful, even though that hadn't been the intent! People want to help; you just need to let them know how they can help you.

I've been in the health and fitness industry now for more than twenty-five years. Over that time, I've seen how, despite our collaborative strengths, women are unfortunately poorly represented in leadership positions. I believe that the larger import of my success is to show other women what is possible. But I also believe that there are real benefits to increasing the number of women in the field. Because women serve as the "health-care CEOs" of their families, they are even more tuned in to receiving health-related information than men, and I am convinced that they would prefer to get this information from other intelligent, reputable women whenever possible.

I'd like to see more women who share a passion for health have the fortitude to push past barriers, crush stereotypes, and create solutions. We are uniquely suited to be the force to change the health of the world if we can join together to do so.

Diana von Welanetz Wentworth is the *New York Times* bestselling author of ten award-winning books and the coauthor of two Chicken Soup for the Soul titles. Film rights to her romantic memoir, *Send Me Someone*, were purchased by the Lifetime Network. With her late husband, Paul von Welanetz, she hosted a long-running television series and founded The Inside Edge (www.InsideEdge.org), a weekly breakfast forum in Southern California that helped launch the careers of many of the most celebrated authors and speakers of our day. After twenty-eight years, progressive business leaders still gather at The Inside Edge to discuss new ideas in psychology, science, global issues, success strategies, spiritual awareness, and the arts. Today, Diana speaks nationally on the subject of her newest book, *Love Your Heart: Follow the Red Thread to a Heart-Centered Life* (written for the American Heart Association).

At seventy, looking back from a more enlightened vantage point, I am able to discern how my deepest childhood wound led to my greatest gift.

My father was fifty when I was born and he suffered from what may have been bipolar disorder (though there was very little understanding of that affliction at the time). My older brother and I were intolerable to him, so when I was eight years old, we were sent away to separate boarding schools, only a few miles from our home. I felt isolated and so alone because the school had only a few other boarders and none in my fourth-grade class. I wondered why I was unacceptable to my own family. And so it was that I developed a lifelong determination to connect deeply and truly.

That goal became my highest priority, and so I chose my two husbands very well. Both my late husband, Paul, and my present husband, Ted, have had a huge capacity for deep partnership. Both perceived and trusted my natural abilities to envision and build community. Both encouraged me, cheered me on, and have been there for me in every possible way through three careers.

Career #1: My mother and grandmother had a deep passion for cooking and gathering people around the table. That passion was so contagious that I left college and attended cooking classes in Paris. After marrying Paul, I continued to study for five years with a renowned chef in Los Angeles. I was a brand-new mother and adjusting to feeling housebound with my baby daughter when Julia Child's television show *The French Chef* introduced French cooking to America. Asking myself how I might attract more people in our lives, I began teaching classes in my home kitchen. I thrived within a community of women gathering around my kitchen table. Soon the classes were in such demand they led to my husband, Paul, joining me as a team in our classes on menus for entertaining. Our first cookbook, *The Pleasure of Your Company*, won the "Cookbook of the Year" award, and that cookbook was followed by five more. We opened our popular cooking school on the Sunset Strip in West Hollywood and hosted a long-running television series, *The New Way Gourmet.*

Career #2: Eight years later, when women were entering the workforce in huge numbers, interest in entertaining at home paled. Trendy restaurants, chef competitions, and one-upmanship took over the cooking world. Paul and I watched our career lose meaning because food no longer served as a catalyst for connection around the home table. Eager and a bit desperate to reinvent our career, Paul and I were drawn to and joined a quite radical motivational coaching group called Impact, led by a woman named Tracey Goss. The group met five days a week from 6 a.m. to 8 a.m. That is where we met people like Tim Piering, Jack Canfield, and Dr. Barbara DeAngelis, who would become our colleagues in the days ahead. Tracey insisted we make far-reaching goals and be accountable for achieving them.

As celebrity chefs, through Impact, we were invited to join a group of leaders in human potential who were traveling into to the Soviet Union (at the height of the Cold War) as "citizen diplomats" to be part of a documentary. It was led by Rama Vernon, founder of *Yoga Journal*, who is known as the "Mother of Yoga" in the United States, as she is the one who first hosted the great yoga master Iyengar in this country. The group included futurist Barbara Marx Hubbard, Patricia Sun, Alan Cohen, the real Patch Adams, Mike Farrell from *M*A*S*H*, Dennis Weaver, and many other leaders and peace activists.

On that trip, we observed how our fellow travelers tended to be loners. By being together during our three-week journey, they began to reach out to create supportive connections and share resources, giving birth to all kinds of new possibilities. Within six months of our return, Paul and I launched The Inside Edge, a weekly motivational breakfast forum where entrepreneurs, professionals, and high-achievers received encouragement and mutual support. It rapidly spread to five Southern California cities. Many of the members, such as Jack Canfield, Louise Hay, and the late author Susan Jeffers, credit The Inside Edge with launching their careers.

Besides hosting the weekly breakfast meetings, Paul and I created futuristic parties and invited members to show up as who they dreamed they would become in the next five years, and spend the evening sharing inspiring stories of how they achieved their success. Paul and I were still gathering people around the table but for a greater purpose. Behaving as though their ambitions were fully achieved, people were transformed! And the ripples that began at The Inside Edge spread way beyond anything we will ever know or imagine. After five vibrant years, though, Paul was diagnosed with terminal cancer. He told me as he was dying, "I don't want you to be alone!" I asked him to send me someone. He soon did and I found myself remarried to Ted Wentworth.

Because of lasting friendships developed through The Inside Edge (www.InsideEdge.org), Jack Canfield and Mark Victor Hansen invited me to become their first coauthor in the hugely successful Chicken Soup for the Soul series. Editing and compiling such heartfelt stories led me beyond cookbooks into the publication of a memoir and other nonfiction.

Career #3: My husband Ted Wentworth and I have begun exploring what we call "Act III." We are trusting that by very consciously embarking on the final chapters of our lives, the true meaning and legacy we have created will be revealed. Staying in our comfortable life and our cozy little home, we risked becoming "pot bound." Now we have liquidated most of our possessions and are heading off on a one-year adventure to explore where we want to land. We sense it will be as part of a very conscious community of like-minded and forward-thinking people in which we can encourage others and share life experience.

I've been truly sparked by women who take hardship and use it to create something exquisite. My best friend, Mary Olsen Kelly, author of *Chicken Soup for the Breast Cancer Survivor's Soul* and many

other titles, wrote her beautiful breast cancer story, *Path of the Pearl.*
She likens a woman's life to that of the pearl oyster that embraces
the irritant that invades it and transforms it into a gem of great value
and beauty. In 2009, I had an opportunity to do that one more time
when I had a sudden heart attack. Thanks to research funded by the
American Heart Association, I had stent surgery and was out of the
hospital in only thirty-six hours. What followed was a year or so of
re-centering, during which I was inspired to write my newest book,
Love Your Heart: Follow the Red Thread to a Heart-Centered Life. In the
book, I share a profound exercise I learned in a coaching session
with Sheva Carr, founding director of The Institute of HeartMath's
HeartMastery Program. Sheva, who teaches the intelligence of the
heart, suggested I create a list on the left side of a piece of paper of
the people who most inspire me, who I would consider "my mentors." I felt stumped at first, and it took a few minutes for my mind
to begin identifying them. Then it began to be fun, and as my list
grew to about ten, I was intrigued to find that almost all of them were
women. There were mostly writers I knew through their books, one
political leader, one film star, my best friend Mary, Oprah Winfrey,
and Helen Keller.

She then guided me in listing the core values each of them
embody/radiate next to their names. Tuning into the essence of each
of these great women, I noticed how my heart seemed to fill with
their admirable qualities: expansiveness, inclusivity, reinvention, elo-
quence, transcendence, devotion, enlightenment, presence, warmth,
care for others, graciousness, beauty, elegance, vulnerability, depth,
surrender, wonder, enthusiasm, and exuberance. Sheva explained
that I had just discovered my own core values through this exercise,
and those qualities still ring true today.

The word that resonated most was *reinvention*. I had chosen
women who, in finding themselves blindsided by difficult circumstances, had discovered ways to become someone entirely new. And
I could see the truth of that in my own life. My mother and my

grandmother had modeled for me the old adage "When life gives you lemons, make lemonade." I had even structured my book *Send Me Someone*, a romantic memoir, based on how the pivotal points of my life were opportunities to transform adversity into new beginnings.

Reflecting on the shock of 2009—the heart attack and surgery—and on the amazing grace of a rapid recovery that found me trekking through the ancient city of Ephesus in Turkey only three weeks later, I am filled with wonder and appreciation for the growth and beauty that year brought. Through it, I learned that one out of three women will die of heart disease and that there was an opportunity for me to help change that. It led me to listen closely to my heart and reinvent my life in many new ways, most meaningfully as an activist and spokesperson for the American Heart Association.

All the vitality and strength that I've gained as a result of my lifestyle changes offer me new opportunities to live long and leave a legacy. Because of that heart attack, I became all the more determined to celebrate every moment, and all the more determined to share this commitment with others.

What is holding you back from embracing manageable changes to give birth to new ways of being? What if we develop a whole new attitude toward the aging process and celebrate every month the new ways we have improved our path?

Ask yourself, "What is my optimal future? How can I define and move fully into it?" Even more important, "What does the world need from me right now?" Might you present radical new ideas to cultivate connection, community, collaboration, continuity, and contribution? Please join me in picking up this bright thread that promises to lead us together into a future full of reinvention and new beginnings!

Kate White is an internationally known expert on leadership and success and a *New York Times* bestselling author of several influential books on work and careers, including, most recently, *I Shouldn't Be Telling You This: How to Ask for the Money, Snag the Promotion, and Create the Career You Deserve* and *Why Good Girls Don't Get Ahead…But Gutsy Girls Do: Nine Secrets Every Career Woman Must Know.* Her advice is based on her extraordinary career running five major magazines. For fourteen years, she was the editor-in-chief of *Cosmopolitan*, the bestselling monthly magazine on the newsstand during her tenure.

Kate is also the author of the *New York Times* bestselling Bailey Weggins mystery series and two stand-alone thrillers, *Hush* and *The Sixes.* Her next novel, a psychological suspense thriller called *Eyes on You*, is scheduled for release in June 2014.

Kate is the winner of the Matrix Award for Outstanding Achievement in Communication, and the Woodhall Institute Award for Ethical Leadership. She speaks around the country and appears frequently on television, including the *Today Show*, to talk about success, leadership, and career issues.

I write suspense novels as well as nonfiction books about success, careers, and leadership, but prior to that I had a long career as the editor-in-chief of women's magazines, including *Cosmopolitan*. It was also a really, really fun place to work, almost like being on a television show (but even better because I had total access to the *Cosmo* beauty closet!).

I think women should go after anything they want professionally, and today there are so many doors open and far fewer restrictions than in the past, but part of the reason I chose women's magazines back in the 1970s was because there were more opportunities for women in that arena than at other types of magazines. I briefly worked at a "co-ed" magazine; my former boss there later told me that I had been denied a position because I was a woman. I decided to go back into the field of women's magazines and that proved to be a good switch for me during those years. It was just easier for me to get to the top that way.

One strategy that's helped me be successful, I think, is a willingness to always keep the big picture in mind and not get so caught up in the details that I lose track of it. There's an old expression that goes, "When you're up to your ass in gnats and alligators, it's easy to forget that your initial objective was to drain the swamp." That sums up work beautifully. No matter what your job is, you have to spend a lot of time killing the alligators—meaning the day-to-day stuff that helps us get by. But in order to be truly successful, you also need to focus on draining the swamp, on making progress toward your long-term goals. No matter how crazy busy I am, I try to book time each week to focus on the big picture. Interestingly, this has also helped in my personal life, giving me a chance me to reflect on my priorities and whether I'm making enough time for my family, my friends, and myself.

I'm also a big believer in research and information gathering. It's critical to learn from your mistakes and dare to look at facts that seem negative at first but can lead to key changes. Knowledge is power, so don't run away from truth. Learn to deal with it.

When young women ask me for practical career advice, I try to impress on them the importance of being gutsy. By that, I mean breaking the rules, taking risks, and not being afraid to ask for what they want. One of my books is titled *Why Good Girls Don't Get Ahead...But Gutsy Girls Do.* Many of us have "good girl" instincts—those can be tough to burn off—but it's important to recognize that taking smart risks and asking for what you want are what ultimately bring success. Admittedly, it can be scary at first. You might be afraid of the possible ramifications, but the more you try it, the more you'll see it pays off. Oh, and let me say that when they offer you a job and they throw out the starting salary, *always* ask for more. Say you'd love the job, but you were hoping for *x* amount instead of *y*. Feel *entitled* to that great salary.

And yet, I should add that though fearlessness is essential, I also think our instinctive female skills are very valuable—like being intuitive, collaborative, empathetic, and good listeners. I've never felt that I had to act tough just to prove my competence. Instead, I've tried to connect with people and bring in a level of caring that seems authentic to me. There was a time when it was harder for women to do that, and there are probably still fields in which women conclude that they must be super-aggressive. Some of the women I've interviewed who work on Wall Street or in male-dominated corporate settings say they've had to downplay their feminine traits, but fortunately in my fields—women's magazines and book publishing—that hasn't been required. There's been no need to be a hard ass (though at times, when someone has worked my last nerve, I've sure been tempted). In so many situations in both work and life, cool works better than hot. If you come out with your guns blazing, it can backfire.

I've had great female bosses and great male bosses, but I have to admit that the female bosses had wonderful skills the guys just didn't possess. My female bosses, for instance, were brilliant listeners, and it's seductive to work with someone like that.

Today, it seems there's far more respect given to what you bring to your career as a woman. Many female skills that were discouraged in the past are now seen as essential—like listening and being collaborative. Studies today show that those are the skills that make excellent managers.

In general, I've loved working with women. At the five magazines I ran, I had a predominantly female staff. I am very grateful for their authenticity, empathy, friendship, and the way they made the workplace joyous and fun. They all helped me in ways they probably didn't even realize.

Sometimes the smallest gestures can have a profound effect. I'm thinking of one in particular that saved me a long time ago. I was about twenty-nine and my boss, who hated public speaking, asked me to give a talk in his place at our company's huge management conference. He insisted that it would boost my career, but what he really wanted to do was have fun at the conference and not worry about giving a speech in front of hundreds of people. Nice, right?

It was one of the first speeches that I gave, and though I rehearsed my butt off, five minutes into it, I knew I was god-awful. I was so scared my lips stuck together like Velcro. All of a sudden, I noticed that a major female publisher in the audience seemed to be hanging on every word I said. She looked positively enraptured and that relaxed me. Why would she do that? Because she saw it as a part of her role in paying it forward. She wanted to help me get through the experience positively—an amazing moment of one woman giving to another, a stranger. What she did in reaching out that day had a great impact on my career. (By the way, I took lots of public speaking classes after that and now love it.)

We need to pay it forward with other women. And we should not only be mentors but sponsors, opening doors for women and making introductions. Research shows that men get promotions more from mentors because their mentors are actually sponsors. We should do the same for women.

I've talked a lot about women in general and tossed out some specific advice, but there are a few things I feel I should add that are important across the board. I would advise anyone starting out, male or female, to give a lot of thought to what their brand or specialty will be. You don't have to carve it in stone right away, but you need to begin to develop an area of expertise. It's also important to gauge your progress. Look at the career arcs of other people in your line of work and note when they hit certain marks. This may help you realize when it's time for you to move on to a new stage of your career. When you are the happiest at your job, it often means you've become too comfortable, and it may be time for a fresh challenge. Be the relentless architect of your career.

Finally, show your gratitude to those who help you. There are a lot of people in Generation Y who don't always say thank you. When someone does a professional favor for you, show your appreciation. A written note. Maybe even a bottle of wine! The person who assisted you will remember that you did so. And she'll remember if you don't.

Nelly Yusupova is a web technology specialist, consultant, strategist, and sought-after speaker. She is the chief technology officer of Webgrrls International, a women's networking organization committed to embracing the technology that will enhance members' personal and professional lives.

Nelly has been at the forefront of the women's movement online since 1999. She is responsible for building and maintaining the technical infrastructure of the organization that supports Webgrrls International's 100 chapters in the United States and around the world.

Through DigitalWoman.com, Nelly also works with entrepreneurs to teach them how to use and leverage technology in their businesses.

As a speaker and corporate trainer, she has keynoted and participated as a speaker, moderator, and panelist at many industry events throughout the United States. She conducts workshops and seminars on technology, social media, blogging, and effective Internet strategies.

In some ways, it is great to be a woman technology expert. There are very few in my line of work and we are in high demand. Opportunities abound. But the scarcity of women in my field can work both for and against me. It's empowering to know that I have entered my industry and participated at the same level as my male colleagues; there is no limit to what I can do and no one who can put a glass ceiling over my head. But there are fewer woman-to-woman connections that I can make professionally, and that can be isolating at times.

I wish there were more women in the computer industry in particular because I think women bring a different perspective, a feminine perspective, to software development. Women often can create software that is, perhaps, more intuitive. And women are always looking for tools that help them save time. When I develop software, I look first at how intuitive the functionality is and I always try to improve it.

Growing up, I had to adopt a "never fear what you don't know" attitude in both my personal and professional lives. When I was thirteen, my family fled from Tajikistan to the United States and I was forced to learn a new language and culture. Then in college, I decided to study computer science without knowing anything about computers. I took eighteen to twenty-one credits per semester, took summer courses, and worked full time. I earned my degree in three years instead of four. I learned fast and it wasn't easy, but I found success because in each new situation, I wasn't intimidated by new information, new tools, or new ideas. I refused to give up simply because I didn't know something!

Because I work in a very male-dominated environment, I just "bring it" and hope that my colleagues, male or female, can keep up. I approach work and professionalism with a very measured and studied approach. I have put in the work and the time, and I have the experience. I plan and then plan more. When you plan well and thoroughly, you can usually do things right, faster the first time, and with no need to do them again. If you plan well, then the execution is easy. Mistakes are costly and no entrepreneur can afford too many of them. Planning alleviates them. I am content knowing that I am very good at what I do.

I believe it's very important to celebrate what you do. Celebrate your victories and share your achievements. Let others know what you are doing and how you do it. Mentor, teach, and inspire those around you.

Never fear what you don't know. And certainly don't fear success. Always revel in your achievements and give kudos to others who achieve their goals. Don't envy, emulate—and success is yours for the taking.

Claire Zammit, PhD, is the cocreator of the acclaimed Feminine Power courses, leading a thriving global community of more than 200,000 women from more than 100 countries. In the last three years, more than 10,000 women have graduated from her seven-week online Feminine Power courses, leadership trainings, and coaching certifications. She is also the cofounder of Evolving Wisdom, a company specializing in online transformative education, which was recently recognized by *Inc.* magazine as one of the top 100 fastest growing companies in America. Claire is a member of Deepak Chopra's Evolutionary Leaders Forum, as well as Jack Canfield's Transformational Leadership Council. She is the author of the forthcoming book *Feminine Power*.

There are important qualities that women bring to organizations and others that are more common to men. Men and women can cultivate *all* these qualities in themselves, but we need to recognize each other's natural strengths and weaknesses and make best use of the former.

I think women have an intuitive and natural advantage in bringing cohesion to things—bringing all the different elements together, getting all the people working on a project together and connected, and generating power that is greater than the sum of its parts. It's a kind of magic that happens. I have seen many women who are naturally good at doing this, and I think it's where the world is headed. In business, science, and technology, there is new emphasis on bringing people together, on building communities as a better way of igniting imagination and creativity.

There is a desire to care for and be of service to people that comes easily and naturally for women in leadership. I think women value relationships more than task and efficiency, that we are more tuned into seeing people's potential and wanting to nurture and support that potential. I think men are more oriented to getting things done but often without this intuitive insight into people's potential, their personal needs, and the social factors that create cohesion in an organization. One of women's weaknesses can be difficulty in balancing all that with the structural things one needs to be successful—the operational functions that are traditionally more masculine endeavors. I think the challenge for women is to integrate these typically masculine and feminine systems of power.

I've seen this in my own career. Years ago, I started running a business with another woman. Neither of us was naturally oriented toward accounting and organizational structure, so things were in disarray. You can't run a successful business or organization without sound processes and structural foundation. It was important to recognize that I couldn't serve all those functions myself. I needed people, women *and* men, who had the right sets of skills and passion for areas in which I was weak. I am proud to see where my organization is now because of the leadership that other people on our team have brought.

Given all that, it's probably no wonder that women make up about 85 percent of the people who come to personal growth workshops like the ones I lead. Over the three years since we founded my current business, we've had seven thousand women in my main online community. I see something waking up in women—they want to actualize their greatest gifts. My partner and I are working together to help create a culture for women and by women.

Evolving Wisdom, a company specializing in online transformative education that my husband and I founded, was recently ranked eighty-third on *Inc.* magazine's list of 500 fastest-growing companies. In the last three years, our full-time staff has grown from zero to fifty. In those three years, I have found a new way to lead that is unique and true to me. The two of us are trying to find new ways of creating organizations that have heart-centered, spiritual values. The fact that I'm a woman—being naturally good at forging new relationships, taking initiative, and being creative—has been a key factor in our success and in building the culture of our organization.

The focus I've always had on cultivating relationships and connections has been a secret to my personal success. I think of success as an authentic expression of who I am and what I care about, so having holistic success in your life grows out of being connected to yourself and others. That has been foundational for me. I made a decision about fifteen years ago to do whatever I needed to make a contribution to the world—to get the best mentoring and to go wherever I needed to go, even when that meant leaving my home in Australia. That's being true to one's calling. The other key to success is forging great connections with people who can support you and teach you and help you. There are women who have been truly critical to my career by extending themselves to me at critical times—such as Dr. Jean Houston, Marianne Williamson, Marci Shimoff, and Katherine Woodward Thomas, who are extraordinary women leaders. I am in awe of how generous these women have been. I absolutely owe so much of my success to them.

One of the hardest things for a woman starting out in any field is to believe in herself. I certainly had a lot of insecurity. I wasn't sure that what I had to contribute to the marketplace was valuable. I was putting myself out there as an expert, despite the fact that I was far from having everything figured out. (I still am.) So having women who can share their own experiences is vital. They can help you see that you don't need to be perfect to make a contribution or to begin your journey in creating a successful enterprise. Advice, mentoring, support—they're all vital to women who are stepping into leadership roles.

And that's advice I'd pass on to any woman getting started. Each of us needs to recognize that we have gifts and talents that the world perhaps has never seen before and may never see again. You should absolutely trust your sense of the contribution you have to give. You should commit completely to finding out what you can create. Once you make that commitment, all manner of unforeseen support will emerge, and you will find your way. Invest in your education and get the best mentoring you possibly can. Find and build support for your enterprise; don't do it all by yourself. Find other women who are as committed to creating their own futures as you are, and support each other on the journey.

The California Women's Conference

WOMEN NETWORK

GLOBAL WOMEN FOUNDATION

JOIN THE MOVEMENT

You are cordially invited to the California Women's Conference! Please enjoy 10% off a General Admission ticket to both days of the conference with promo code: WOMENCHANGETHEWORLD

Thank you for supporting the California Women's Conference, the premiere women's conference in the United States. The California Women's Conference offers its attendees inspiration, resources, and connections to take the next step in business, personal development, health and wellness, or philanthropic endeavors. Featuring widely respected thought leaders, talented entertainers, and a marketplace of ideas, exhibits, networking and panel discussions. The conference is designed to benefit women from all walks of life.

www.CaliforniaWomensConfererence.com

JOIN THE MOVEMENT ON SOCIAL MEDIA

facebook California Womens Conference

twitter CaWomensConf